GOOD HOUSEKEEPING

CREATIVE
FOOD PROCESSOR
COOKERY

GOOD HOUSEKEEPING

CREATIVE FOOD PROCESSOR COOKERY

NICOLA COX

THE
LEISURE
CIRCLE

This edition specially produced for
The Leisure Circle Ltd
by Ebury Press
Division of the National Magazine Company Ltd
Colquhoun House
27–37 Broadwick Street
London W1V 1FR

First Impression 1986

Edited by Veronica Sperling and Caroline Schuck
Designed by Bill Mason
Illustrations by Linda Smith
Photography by Paul Kemp
Styling by Jane Kemp
Cookery by Susanna Tee and Maxine Clark

Filmset by Advanced Filmsetters (Glasgow) Ltd.
Printed and bound in Italy by New Interlitho, S.p.a., Milan

CONTENTS

Acknowledgements
All books are teamwork and this is no exception. My
thanks go not only to all the Ebury Press team for their
tireless and professional work but to my students, to
our secretary, Mrs James, and to to my husband Simon
who have respectively cooked endlessly, typed
accurately and proof-read unstintingly, to help to
make this a book that we all hope you will really enjoy.

Farthinghoe 1985   Nicola Cox

INTRODUCTION

Having a food processor saves time and once the basic techniques have been mastered it can be used in an exciting and creative way to produce elaborate dishes with ease.

I have created the recipes in this book to increase your repertoire and give you new and unusual ideas, many of which have been devised with healthy eating in mind. Some are totally my own creation, born from working with my processor; others, like Hummus, Koftas and Pitta Bread (pages 19, 34 and 86), are world classics which I have adapted for the machine.

There are many machines with different characteristics taking varying times to do the same job, so in the recipes I have concentrated on describing the textures to achieve rather than the length of time to process. As well as the basic metal blade, slicer, grater and plastic blade, I have used the more usual and available additional blades. Personally, I find the whisk attachment the least successful; and so have suggested, throughout, using a hand whisk as an alternative. I have concentrated on recipes that use various blades to their best advantage, and explored different preparation techniques, to show you the machine's real creative powers. In some cases this can produce totally new results either not previously possible or at least very difficult to achieve.

I have found it exciting to write this book and I hope you may find it both stimulating to read and an aid to creating your own recipes. I hope that you will enjoy yourself expanding the ideas that I have suggested and, if so, I will feel my job was well done.

TIPS FOR GETTING THE BEST FROM YOUR FOOD PROCESSOR

- for evenly sliced foods, pack tightly in the feed tube e.g. carrots, some fat end up, some fat end down
- slightly soft vegetables, e.g. cucumber and aubergine, that appear to be too thick to fit the feed tube can be gently squeezed and moulded to fit the shape
- to change the thickness of foods, vary the pressure on the plunger
- chop in small quantities, especially meat
- to help soften butter for processing, pour hot water on to the bowl with metal blade in position, leave for 1 minute, drain and dry before adding butter
- when chopping herbs, it helps to add some liquid to the bowl
- to pour liquid mixtures from the bowl, slip a finger up the central column and hold the blade in place by pressing it firmly against the central column. This allows the bowl to be tipped without the blade falling out
- it is useful to keep two metal blades; one for general use and a sharp one specially for meat
- a second bowl is useful e.g. when your first is full of pâté mixture and you have forgotten to chop the parsley or make the breadcrumbs
- when emptying thick mixtures from the bowl, scrape out as much as you can, return the bowl to the machine, process for a moment and the remaining mixture will fly off the blades so it's easy to scrape out

COOKERY NOTES

Follow either metric or imperial measures for the recipes in this book as they are not interchangeable. Size 3 eggs should be used unless otherwise stated.

SOUPS

You can use your food processor to create soups in moments. And with the help of different blades, vegetables can be processed in a variety of ways to make a whole range of textures from velvet smooth to rustic rough, through chopped, sliced, shredded and chunky. Take care not to chop raw vegetables too finely or they will become watery or pulpy and will not fry or sweat properly. Their enzymes will also be released and you will get a bitter and unpleasantly strong flavour.

To achieve the smoothest texture it's best to process the soup ingredients with the liquid strained off at first, unlike using a blender which works best with a more liquid mixture.

SHRIMP BISQUE

Tiny shrimps, which are such a business to peel, can be made into a rich and tasty bisque with the food processor doing all the pounding and pulverising for you. Cooked rice and egg yolks are used to thicken this soup. Rice usually doubles in weight when cooked, so you will need 50 g (2 oz) of uncooked rice for this recipe. *Serves 4–6.*

1 onion, skinned
1–2 cloves garlic
50 g (2 oz) butter
225 g (8 oz) shrimps in their
    shells
150 ml ($\frac{1}{4}$ pint) dry white wine
900 ml (1$\frac{1}{2}$ pints) fish stock or
    water and 1 fish stock cube
1 bay leaf
3–4 parsley stalks
1 sprig thyme
100 g (4 oz) cooked rice
about 2.5 ml ($\frac{1}{2}$ tsp) tomato purée
pinch of mace
pepper
300 ml ($\frac{1}{2}$ pint) milk
a few parsley heads
2 egg yolks
150 ml ($\frac{1}{4}$ pint) cream
salt

USING THE METAL BLADE: cut up the onion and garlic into the bowl and process with the on/off or pulse technique until finely chopped. Melt the butter in a large casserole or pan, add the processed onion and garlic and cook gently until soft.

Process the unpeeled shrimps until they are very finely chopped and add to the onion and garlic in the pan; sauté for several minutes. Add the wine and boil fast for several minutes to reduce. Add the stock or water and fish stock cube, bay leaf, parsley stalks, thyme, rice, tomato purée, mace and pepper. Simmer, uncovered, for 30–40 minutes, skimming off any froth that might form. Drain off all the liquid into a lipped bowl and reserve.

USING THE METAL BLADE: process the solids for 1–2 minutes until well pulverised and then gradually add some of the reserved stock with the engine running. Pass this bisque through a large, fine mesh sieve pressing the debris well and adding in the reserved liquid and the milk. For extra flavour, you can reprocess the debris with the liquid that has passed through the sieve and resieve. Reheat the soup.

USING THE METAL BLADE: chop the parsley finely then add the egg yolks and cream and process until well mixed. Take about 300 ml ($\frac{1}{2}$ pint) of the hot soup and, with the engine running, pour it down the feed tube in a fine trickle, adding a speck more tomato purée if the soup is not an appetising colour. Return the mixture to the pan. Season to taste with salt. Heat the bisque very gently, until it thickens, without allowing it to boil or the yolks might curdle. Check the seasoning and serve.

FISH SOUP WITH ROUILLE

The pounded and strained fish soups of Provence, with their intricate flavours, are justly famous and the subject of much holiday nostalgia. Now, with a food processor (one of the larger and sturdier models is advisable for this dish) to pound and pulverise the fish they are not too laborious to reproduce. They are served with *rouille*, a rust-coloured garlic, chilli and saffron mayonnaise, which is easy to make in the food processor. Although you cannot buy all the varieties of Mediterranean fish here, there is enough choice to give a wonderfully tasty broth. All sorts of bits and pieces will do for you don't really need much flesh. For a really authentic flavour, don't bother to gut any small fish like red mullet. *Serves 4–6.*

---

50 ml (2 fl oz) good quality olive oil

2–3 onions, skinned

900 g–1.4 kg (2–3 lb) mixed really fresh fish such as: small monkfish, red mullet, gurnard, cod cheeks, a small piece of mackerel, conger eel, huss, skate or whitebait. Also, if possible, some squid and a few prawns in their shells

400 g (14 oz) can tomatoes

at least 3–4 cloves garlic or up to a head, peeled

3–4 stalks of fennel or 4 ml ($\frac{3}{4}$ tsp) fennel seeds

good sprig thyme

1 bay leaf

4–6 long parsley stalks, flat leafed for choice

1–2 packets of saffron or generous pinch saffron threads

salt

pepper

pinch of cayenne

ROUILLE

1 packet saffron or pinch saffron threads

1 slice bread

2 cloves garlic

1 egg yolk

1–2.5 ml ($\frac{1}{4}$–$\frac{1}{2}$ tsp) cayenne pepper or hot chilli powder

5 ml (1 tsp) mild paprika

60–90 ml (4–6 tbsp) tomato purée

100 ml (4 fl oz) olive oil

salt

TO SERVE

slices of French bread

grated Gruyère or Parmesan cheese (optional)

Using a wide-based, heavy pan heat the olive oil.

USING THE STANDARD SLICING DISC: slice the onions and add to the olive oil. Cook over a moderate heat until golden, toss in the fish, washed and gutted if you wish, whole or in pieces as seems appropriate. Add the tomatoes, garlic, fennel, thyme, bay leaf and parsley stalks and mix well. Cook for 10 minutes so the fish exude their juices and keep stirring frequently to prevent burning. Now add 2–2.4 litres ($3\frac{1}{2}$–4 pints) of water, the saffron, salt and pepper. Boil vigorously, uncovered, for 20–30 minutes. The fish should break up and the oil should amalgamate with the liquid. Strain off the liquid. Pick out any herbs, backbones or heavy bones which might be too much for the processor.

USING THE METAL BLADE: process the contents of the pan until very well chopped and pulverised (you will probably need to do this in several batches), adding in some of the reserved liquid as you process. Either put the resulting pulpy mixture through a mouli-légume, an excellent way of getting the tasty liquid separated from the debris and bones, or press through a coarse strainer and wring out the debris in a cloth. Return the soup to the pan, adjust the seasoning, adding a pinch of cayenne.

To make the *rouille*: soak the saffron in about 60 ml (4 tbsp) of the hot fish soup.

USING THE METAL BLADE: process the bread and garlic until finely chopped; add the yolk, cayenne pepper, paprika and tomato purée. Then with the machine running, gradually add the oil and saffron stock to make a smooth mayonnaise-style sauce. Turn into a bowl.

Dry off the slices of French bread in a slow oven 150°C (300°F) mark 2 until crisp and light brown. Reheat the soup. Serve it with the croûtes, grated cheese and *rouille* handed round separately. Guests can spread the *rouille* on the croûtes and float them on the soup or whisk some into their soup with a fork, depending on their taste.

CHICKEN AND VEGETABLE SOUP WITH FORCEMEAT BALLS

This chicken soup, thick with vegetables and chicken and served with forcemeat balls makes an excellent main meal soup in the old English fashion. The stock can be used in other dishes as can the chicken meat. You can vary the vegetables according to the season. In summer, peas, beans, courgettes and tomatoes can be used. Noodles or rice can be added in place of, or as well as, the potatoes, and fresh chopped herbs give it a lovely finish. Dried *cèpes* mushrooms, called *porcini* in Italian shops, give this soup an interesting flavour. *Serves 4–6 as a main dish.*

1.6 kg (3½ lb) chicken with giblets
1 large onion, skinned
3–4 carrots, peeled
1 stick celery, trimmed and cleaned
1 leek, washed
2 medium potatoes, peeled
50 g (2 oz) turnip or parsnip, peeled (optional)
1 clove garlic, skinned
bouquet garni of 4–6 parsley stalks, sprig thyme, 1 bayleaf, 2 cloves and 4–6 peppercorns
1 chicken stock cube
2–3 pieces dried *cèpes* mushrooms (optional)
salt

FORCEMEAT BALLS
75 g (3 oz) brown or white bread
2–3 mushrooms (optional)
a few heads parsley
sprigs celery leaf (optional)
a little grated lemon rind
pinch of mace
2.5 ml (½ tsp) salt
pepper
30 ml (2 tbsp) chicken fat or butter, melted
1 egg
30–45 ml (2–3 tbsp) oil, for frying

TO GARNISH
handful parsley heads

Remove any chunks of fat from inside the chicken. Reserve the fat and render it. Reserve it and use for the forcemeat balls. Put the chicken into a saucepan of boiling water, boil for 1 minute and drain, discarding the water. Rinse the pan, return the chicken and cover with 2.6 litres (4½ pints) of cold water.

USING THE THICKEST SLICING DISC (6 mm): cut the onion into four, lengthways, stack upright in the feed tube and slice with medium firm pressure. Cut the carrots into halves, quarters or sixths lengthways depending on their girth, stack upright and slice with firm pressure. Stack the feed tube with the celery and leek and slice with medium pressure. Cut the potatoes and turnip in half lengthways then each half into 3–4 lengthways strips; stack upright and slice with firm pressure. Add all this to the pan with the chicken. Add the garlic, bouquet garni, stock cube, *cèpes* and the salt. Bring to the simmer, skim off any frothy scum that forms and simmer gently, uncovered, for 30–40 minutes or until the chicken is cooked. Remove the chicken. Once the vegetables are all tender, remove the giblets, bouquet garni and about 300 ml (½ pint) of the stock if you feel there is too much; adjust the seasoning. Using absorbent kitchen paper, degrease the stock. Chop up some of the meat into chunks and add to the soup. Reserve the rest of the meat for other dishes.

USING THE METAL BLADE: make the forcemeat balls. Break the bread into the food processor, leaving the crusts on if they are fresh. Add the mushrooms, if using, parsley heads and celery leaves, a little grated lemon rind, mace, salt and pepper. Process to coarse crumbs; trickle over the chicken fat or melted butter, add an egg and process just to mix but do not over process. Form into 12 balls with your hands. Heat the oil in a frying pan and, when hot, fry the balls in it until brown all over.

USING THE METAL BLADE: chop the parsley, adding 30–45 ml (2–3 tbsp) of the stock to help it chop evenly. Stir it into the soup. Add the forcemeat balls and serve.

VELVET LIMEY SOUP

Make this variation of Greek *avgolemono* soup when you have some really good game, duck, turkey, chicken or fish stock. It is sharply limey and has a wonderful texture. Do not use an aluminium pan to cook it in as the lime will react with the metal and the egg yolks will discolour. *Serves 4–6.*

1.5–1.7 litres (2⅓–3 pints) very good stock
30 ml (2 tbsp) uncooked long grain rice
2 eggs
1–2 limes
handful parsley heads

Using a non-aluminium pan, gently simmer the rice in the stock for 20–30 minutes; if necessary, leave half uncovered so it reduces and strengthens.

USING THE METAL BLADE: process the eggs with 15 ml (1 tbsp) of cold water until light and frothy; add the juice of 1½ limes and process again. Strain about 300 ml (½ pint) of the soup into a jug. With the machine running, very gradually pour this hot soup down the feed tube. Return almost all the soup to the pan and throw the parsley heads in with the last few spoonfuls of soup in the food processor; process until finely chopped and add to the soup. Return the soup to a very gentle heat and heat gently, stirring, until the soup has thickened. Do not boil. Check the seasoning and add more lime if need be. It should be quite sharp. Serve. I often leave this soup beside the stove, or in a bain-marie filled with warm water 40–45°C (100–110°F), for quite a while to let the soup thicken gently. If disaster strikes and the soup starts to curdle, pour it immediately, without the rice, into the running processor which will usually reamalgamate it. Take care not to over-fill the machine in your panic!

CREAM OF CELERIAC SOUP

Here is a cream soup made without cream! Often you may want to enrich a soup for a special occasion, but there is no cream handy. This is easy with a food processor; the secret lies in adding a nut of butter as you process it to enrich and enhance its flavour. Unlike with cream, you can reheat the soup and even boil it without it separating out. Celeriac makes a lovely winter soup. *Serves 4–6.*

1 large celeriac root, about 450 g (1 lb)
1 small onion, skinned
50 g (2 oz) butter
900 ml (1½ pints) chicken stock or water and 1 stock cube
salt
pepper
5 ml (1 tsp) potato flour
150 ml (¼ pint) milk
25–75 g (1–3 oz) butter, to enrich

USING THE CHIPPER DISC OR THICK SLICING DISC: cut the celeriac into slices the width of the feed tube and then peel. If using the slicing disc, cut the slices into narrow columns before stacking the feed tube so you don't get large slices and process with firm pressure on the plunger; also process the onion. Melt the butter in a heavy pan, add the celeriac and onion and stir until coated in butter. Cook gently, covered, stirring from time to time for 10–15 minutes without browning. Add the stock, season and simmer for about 15–20 minutes until completely tender. Mix the potato flour with the cold milk, add and simmer, stirring, for 1–2 minutes. Drain off all the liquid into a lipped bowl and reserve.

USING THE METAL BLADE: process the solids until absolutely smooth then, with the motor still running, add in the butter for enriching and some of the reserved liquid. Switch off and return the soup through a large sieve to the rinsed out pan. Pour the remaining liquid into the sieve to help the soup through. Adjust the seasoning, reheat and serve.

ICED CARIBBEAN AVOCADO SOUP

This is a recipe I created using the fresh ingredients of the Caribbean. It is very light and has a wonderful flavour. You can get all the ingredients here but check that they are fresh. When buying coconuts make sure they are crack free and don't have any mould growing on them. Shake them; they should be heavy with milk. It is a wise precaution to buy an extra coconut just in case one is rancid. Grated fresh coconut freezes very well. *Serves 4–6.*

1 fresh coconut
½ shallot or small onion, skinned
    and sliced
½ clove garlic
1 small fresh chilli or good shake
    of Tabasco or pinch of cayenne
juice of 2–3 limes and a strip of
    thinly peeled lime rind
2 cm (¾ inch) cube peeled fresh
    root ginger
2–3 ripe avocados
5 ml (1 tsp) salt

To make coconut cream: pierce the soft eye of the coconut, drain out and discard (or drink) the liquid. Crack the coconut open and remove all the flesh, prizing it off with an old knife. Taste a bit to make sure it isn't rancid. Using a potato peeler, pare off a few wafer thin slices of coconut and toast them in a moderate oven 180°C (350°F) mark 4 until crisp and golden. Crumble and reserve to use as a garnish.

USING THE METAL BLADE: place all the remaining broken up bits of coconut in the food processor bowl and process with the on/off or pulse technique until very finely chopped. Pour 150 ml (¼ pint) of boiling water over the chopped coconut, process again then turn out into a piece of muslin or cloth and squeeze vigorously to expel all the liquid. Reserve the liquid. Return the coconut to the bowl, process again and add 225 ml (8 fl oz) of boiling water. Turn the coconut into the muslin; squeeze out the liquid and combine it with the first pressing; cover and leave to cool. Discard the coconut residue.

USING THE METAL BLADE: process the shallot, garlic, chilli or Tabasco or cayenne, thinly peeled lime rind and the ginger until chopped and amalgamated. Scrape the flesh from the avocados and add it to the other ingredients; process until absolutely smooth. Add the prepared coconut cream, salt and enough lime juice to give a fresh limey flavour. Strain through a sieve and add up to 450 ml (¾ pint) of cold water to thin the soup to the desired flavour and consistency. Adjust the seasoning to taste. Cover the soup as closely as possible with cling film, pressing it down onto the surface to prevent discoloration. Chill. Ideally, serve within 1 hour or so of making. Hand the toasted coconut shreds round as a garnish.

POTAGE DE LÉGUMES RETROUVÉS

This very simple soup, using left-over cooked vegetables and thickened with mashed potato, is something that I find myself using again and again in endless variations. I give it to you so you know the rough quantities but you can develop it in many different ways, using leftover spinach, celeriac, parsnips, turnip, beans or peas and finishing it off with a little fresh watercress, sorrel, chervil, basil, marjoram or whatever is in season. *Serves 4–6.*

---

250 g (9 oz) cooked carrots
15 ml (1 tbsp) flour (optional)
15 g (½ oz) butter
175 g (6 oz) mashed potato
1 litre (1¾ pints) hot stock or
    water and 1½ stock cubes
salt
pepper
1 bunch watercress or handful
    parsley
150 ml (¼ pint) milk

USING THE METAL BLADE: process the carrots until finely chopped then add the flour (only add this if you have time to let the soup simmer for 20–30 minutes) and the butter (use more for a richer soup, less if the vegetables are very buttery) and the potato; process and add about 300 ml (½ pint) of the hot stock or water. Once well combined, turn into a pan and add the remaining stock or water and cube. Season and simmer for 15–30 minutes.

USING THE METAL BLADE: place the watercress or parsley heads in the bowl and process while you gradually pour in the milk. Once finely chopped, pour into the soup, heat through and serve.

POTATO, APPLE AND PARSNIP IN TOMATO BROTH

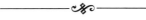

A really chunky soup for winter, using the chipper disc to cut up the potato, apple and parsnip. The slightly sweet-sour taste of this simple soup is rather attractive and I think you will find the basic tomato broth extremely versatile. Any other vegetables, or rice, chicken or pasta can be added to it to make a quick and tasty soup. When tomatoes are plentiful you can use them roughly chopped up to make a broth. Process the broth and strain it before adding the other ingredients. *Serves 4–6.*

---

2 medium onions, skinned
30 ml (2 tbsp) olive oil
45 ml (3 tbsp) tomato purée
1.5 litres (2½ pints) light stock or
    water and 1½ meat or vegetable
    stock cubes
small handful of fresh basil,
    chopped or 2.5 ml (½ tsp) dried
salt
pepper
1 medium cooking apple, peeled
    and cored
1 medium potato, peeled
1 small parsnip, peeled

USING THE FINE SLICING DISC: halve and slice the onions. Heat the oil in a large casserole or pan and fry the onions until soft and golden. Add the tomato purée and continue to fry over a medium heat for several minutes, stirring all the time, until the tomato smells fragrant; then add the stock or water and cube, basil and seasoning and simmer briskly, uncovered, for 20–30 minutes.

USING THE CHIPPER DISC: chip the apple, using medium pressure on the plunger. Chip the potato and parsnip using firm pressure on the plunger. Add to the soup and simmer for 10–20 minutes until tender. Adjust the seasoning, adding a little more basil if necessary. Serve.

BLACK BEAN SOUP

Dark, thick and peasanty, this warm and comforting main meal soup is a great favourite with its zesty chilli-cream croûtes. Try to use Mexican chili powder, which is a blend of chilli, garlic, marjoram and cumin. *Serves 4–6.*

---

1 onion, skinned
1 carrot, peeled
1 stick celery
400 g (14 oz) black beans, washed and soaked overnight
2 stock cubes
1–2 cloves garlic, peeled
45 ml (3 tbsp) tomato purée
2.5–5 ml ($\frac{1}{2}$–1 tsp) Mexican chili powder
salt
a little fresh marjoram or $\frac{1}{4}$ tsp dried marjoram or oregano

TO GARNISH
4–6 slices French bread
oil, for frying (optional)
2 –3 rashers bacon, diced
60–90 ml (4–6 tbsp) whipping cream
salt
pepper
pinch Mexican chili powder
squeeze lemon juice
finely chopped fresh marjoram, chives or parsley

USING THE MEDIUM SLICING DISC: slice the onion, carrot and celery. Drain the soaked beans and put into a large pan with 1.7 litres (3 pints) of water. Add the stock cubes, sliced vegetables, garlic, tomato purée and chili powder. Simmer gently for about 2 hours or until the beans are tender, adding salt and marjoram or oregano when they are nearly done. Drain the liquid from the beans and reserve.

USING THE METAL BLADE: process the beans as smooth as you wish (I like them quite chunky and bitty in this soup) then, with the motor running, add some of the liquid down the feed tube. Return the soup to the pan (you can sieve the soup first if you wish).

Make the garnish: either toast the French bread or fry in oil to make croûtes. Fry the bacon until crisp. Process the cream with a flavouring of salt, pepper, chili powder and lemon juice until just firm but not for longer than about 20 seconds or the cream could curdle. Heap the cream on the hot fried or toasted croûtes and sprinkle with the bacon and chopped herbs.

Reheat the soup, adjust the seasoning and serve. Float a decorated croûte on each helping.
See illustration facing page 16

PÂTÉS, DIPS AND STARTERS

A wide variety of meat, fish and vegetables can all be transformed with a processor into delicious pâtés and dips. Smooth or chunky pâtés can be made in seconds. If you enjoy rich Mediterranean flavours, you will find some exciting new ideas for dips; try Mouamara (page 20) a spicy Cypriot nut dip, or Roasted Pepper and Aubergine Dip (page 18). Both of these can be prepared ahead and served at a party.

In terrines where you would otherwise mince the meat, the food processor chops it without squeezing and pressing as a mincer does and therefore gives a moister and more succulent pâté. However, the meat needs to be carefully trimmed of sinew and gristle.

FISH TERRINE WITH SEVICHED SALMON STRIPES

A delicate white fish mousse, lightly seasoned with lime and ginger, is sandwiched with layers of salmon that has been marinated in lime juice and the terrine can be wrapped in a layer of toasted *nori* seaweed.

The light delicate flavours make this terrine an ideal summer starter. *Serves 4–6.*

MARINATED SALMON
100–175 g (4–6 oz) thinly sliced
 fresh or smoked salmon
salt (optional)
pepper
juice from 1–2 limes

WHITE FISH MOUSSE
225 g (8 oz) whiting fillet
10 ml (2 tsp) gelatine
30 ml (2 tbsp) dry white wine
grated rind and juice of $\frac{1}{2}$–1 lime
a little finely grated fresh root
 ginger
salt
pepper
100 g (4 oz) cream cheese
100 ml (4 fl oz) whipping cream

If using a fresh salmon steak, remove the skin and bone and divide into two. Stand each half upright on a board and cut into very thin slices.

Lay the salmon in a glass bowl. If using fresh salmon, season well with salt and pepper; if smoked, use only pepper. Add lime juice just to cover.

Sprinkle the gelatine over the white wine in a small bowl and leave to swell. Skin and bone the whiting, set in a shallow dish and season with lime rind and juice, a little grated ginger and salt and pepper. Add the soaked gelatine-wine cake, cover closely and cook until just flaking.

USING THE METAL BLADE: flake the whiting into the bowl, removing any bones; process then add in the cooking liquid. Now add the cream cheese and process, stirring down once, for just long enough to amalgamate it (do not process for long or cream cheese may curdle). Correct the seasoning and leave until cold and just thickening. Drain the salmon.

USING THE WHISK ATTACHMENT OR A HAND WHISK: whip the cream until it softly holds its shape; then fold into the thickening fish mousse.

If you wish to, line an oblong 600 ml (1 pint) terrine with a sheet of *nori* seaweed, toasted briefly over a gas flame or under a grill if it is not ready-toasted. Alternatively, line the terrine with Bakewell paper.

Spread a third of the fish mousse in the base and cover with a layer of salmon slices; spread another even layer of fish mousse then salmon and finish with mousse and finally salmon. Leave to set in the fridge for 4–24 hours then turn out and serve, cut into slices with a very sharp wet knife. Dress attractively on plates with a few salad leaves, if liked, and serve with melba toast or crisp thin biscuits.

See illustration facing page 17

LIGHTEST LIVER MOUSSELINE

This light and delicate chicken liver pâté, with its flavouring of Pernod and basil, is often preferred to heavier and richer versions. It can be served with bread or toast, piped into mushroom caps or hollow celery stalks. It is delicious spread under the skin of a chicken breast before roasting. *Serves 4–6.*

25 g (1 oz) butter
1 small onion, skinned and finely chopped
100 g (4 oz) chicken livers
3–4 leaves fresh basil or 2.5 ml ($\frac{1}{2}$ tsp) dried
2.5 ml ($\frac{1}{2}$ tsp) Pernod or vermouth, sherry or brandy
100 g (4 oz) cream cheese
50 ml (2 fl oz) whipping cream
15–30 ml (1–2 tbsp) yogurt
salt
pepper

Melt the butter in a frying pan and add the onion. Cook until softened. Carefully pick over the chicken livers, removing any green-tinged flesh and cut each into 2–3 pieces. Once the onion is soft, turn up the heat, add the livers, and sauté briskly until sealed on the outside. Cover, lower the temperature and continue to cook until done but still rosy in the middle.

USING THE METAL BLADE: turn the liver and onion mixture into the food processor, add the basil and Pernod and process until very smooth. Now add the cream cheese, cream, yogurt and salt and pepper and process briefly, using the on/off or pulse technique and stopping to stir down, until absolutely smooth. Check the seasoning and flavouring and turn into a pot. Serve cold.

MUSHROOM PÂTÉ

In Périgord, *cèpes* mushrooms are often served with a *persillade* of garlic and parsley. There is no doubt that garlic and parsley do have a great affinity with mushrooms of all sorts and I use them in this vegetarian pâté to enhance the mushroom flavour. This pâté will keep well in the fridge and can be used to enliven soups, stews, sauces or as a topping for steaks or chops as well as being a most healthy and tasty first course pâté in its own right. *Serves 4–6.*

1 small onion, skinned and cut up
3–4 cloves garlic, skinned and cut up
50 g (2 oz) butter
a good handful of parsley heads
500 g (1 lb 2 oz) mushrooms
salt
pepper
15 ml (1 tbsp) brandy
30 ml (2 tbsp) Madeira or 45–60 ml (3–4 tbsp) red wine

TO SERVE
1–2 lemons, quartered

USING THE METAL BLADE: add the roughly cut up onion and garlic to the bowl and chop with the on/off or pulse technique until roughly chopped. Melt the butter in a heavy pan, add the onion and soften. Process the parsley until fairly finely chopped, add the mushrooms and process until they too are finely chopped before adding to the pan. Season with salt and pepper and stir in the brandy and the Madeira or wine. Cook over a low heat for about 30 minutes until all the liquid has gone and you cannot press any out of the mass. Taste and pack into pots. Reprocess for a smoother pâté. You may like to process in up to 100 g (4 oz) butter, once the mushroom mixture has cooled slightly, to give a softer creamier pâté. Serve with fresh hot toast or warm Light Brown Bread, Rolled-up Onion Bread or Soft Yogurt Scones (pages 85, 88 and 87). Hand lemon quarters with the pâté.

Black bean soup with chilli cream croûtes (page 14)

Terrine Mélange

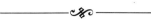

A really good terrine is always useful for a party and I do this one in a long mould from which I can cut 20 slices. I have given a recipe for a large quantity, not only because there are a lot of ingredients and it would be fiddly to do less, but also because this is one of the few terrines that I find freezes well. The reason for it freezing well is because the meats are first well spiced, which draws out their moisture and leaves them well seasoned. Breadcrumbs are added to hold any surplus moisture. Remember to press the terrine well. Freeze it after it has matured and, when defrosting, let it thaw slowly and thoroughly. *Makes up to 20 slices.*

SPICING MIXTURE

5 ml (1 tsp) green peppercorns or 2.5 ml (½ tsp) black

2.5 ml (½ tsp) juniper berries

1–2 cloves garlic, peeled

10 ml (2 tsp) fresh lemon thyme, thyme or sage leaves or 1–2.5 (¼–½ tsp) dried

10 ml (2 tsp) sea salt

45 ml (3 tbsp) gin

1 ml (¼ tsp) quatre épice or allspice

TERRINE

2 crustless slices brown or white bread

30–60 ml (2–4 tbsp) dry white wine

250 g (9 oz) belly of pork, sinew and gristle removed, sliced into 2 or 3 pieces

350 g (12 oz) back pork fat, sliced into 2 or 3 pieces

250 g (9 oz) cooked ham, sliced into 2 or 3 pieces

200 g (7 oz) pie veal, chicken or rabbit meat, cubed

100 g (4 oz) lamb's or pig's liver

2–3 eggs

To make the spicing mix: pound the peppercorns, juniper berries, garlic and herbs to a paste in a mortar and add the salt (more or less depending on how salty the ham is), gin and quatre épice or allspice and mix all together. Rub this mixture well into the sliced chunks of meat. Leave in a cool place for 12–24 hours.

USING THE METAL BLADE: prepare the terrine. Process the bread to crumbs and add enough wine to make the mixture into a paste. Scrape out and set aside.

Remove about a quarter of the fat and half the ham chunks from the spicing mix and dice by hand; reserve. Dice the remaining meats and liver.

USING THE METAL BLADE: drop the meats and liver in small batches with some of the crumb paste onto the moving blades and process until fairly finely minced. Repeat this until all the meat is minced.

USING THE PLASTIC BLADE: return all the mixture to the bowl (in smaller machines this may need to be done in two batches), add the eggs and reserved cubes of ham and fat and process until well mixed. Turn into a long 1.5 litre (2½ pint) mould lined with Bakewell paper; press it well in with wet hands so there are no gaps. Set the terrine in a bain-marie filled with boiling water to come at least halfway up the outside of the mould. Cook, uncovered, in a slow oven 150°C (300°F) mark 2 for 1¼–2 hours. The terrine is cooked when it comes away from the sides of the dish and when a skewer stuck in produces no pink juice.

Leave the terrine to cool then weight it with a 2-kg (4-lb) weight. Keep in a fridge or cold larder for several days before turning out and serving, cut in thin slices.

Fish terrine with seviched salmon stripes (page 15)

SMOKED HADDOCK PÂTÉ

This is an unusual recipe because it uses raw smoked haddock. Use only the best oak-smoked fish; it's really just like using smoked salmon only much cheaper and the flavour is arguably better! *Serves 4–6.*

250 g (9 oz) oak-smoked haddock
pepper
pinch cayenne
juice of $\frac{1}{2}$–1 lemon
1 egg or 30–45 ml (2–3 tbsp)
    yogurt or whipping cream
200 g (7 oz) cream cheese

Carefully skin and de-bone the smoked haddock and cut it into cubes.

USING THE METAL BLADE: process the fish to a fine paste and add the pepper, cayenne, lemon juice, egg, yogurt or cream. Process until smooth then add the cream cheese. Process again, stirring down, but not for too long or the mixture may curdle. Check the seasoning and pass through a sieve or mouli-légume if you want a smoother texture. Turn into a serving dish.

Serve as a pâté with hot toast, rolls or crispbread.

ROASTED PEPPER AND AUBERGINE DIP

Red or green peppers are grilled till their skins blacken; this brings out their flavour and makes them more digestible. Combined with baked aubergine they make an unusual, rich-tasting purée that can be used as a dip, served with Pitta Bread (page 86) or as a vegetable with roasts, grills, kebabs or cold meats. For a really special flavour, cook the vegetables on a barbecue. *Serves 4–6 as a dip or 1–2 as a vegetable.*

1 large aubergine
1–2 cloves garlic, skinned, cut in
    half lengthwise
2 red or green peppers
2.5 ml ($\frac{1}{2}$ tsp) coriander seeds
2.5 ml ($\frac{1}{2}$ tsp) salt
50–75 ml (2–3 fl oz) olive oil
15–30 ml (1–2 tbsp) lemon juice

Make knife slits in the aubergine and tuck in the garlic cloves so that they are well inside. Grease a baking sheet and place the aubergine on it. Bake in a hot oven 220°C (425°F) mark 7 for 20–30 minutes until the aubergine is soft.

Place the peppers directly over a gas flame or under a hot grill and turn as they blacken on one side until their skins are blackened all over and the peppers are softened and cooked. Wash the charred and blackened skins off under a running tap and halve the peppers, removing the seeds and core. While the peppers are cooking, roast the coriander seeds in a heavy dry pan over a medium heat until fragrant and then pound them with a pestle and mortar. Peel the baked aubergines. removing all the skin.

USING THE METAL BLADE: place the prepared aubergine and pepper in the bowl and process to a purée; add the salt and roasted, pounded coriander and, as the machine runs, trickle in the oil which will be absorbed as in a mayonnaise. Adjust the seasoning, add lemon juice to taste and turn into a bowl. Serve warm or cold.

HUMMUS

A simple Middle Eastern dip made from chick peas and tahina. Tahina, a sesame paste, is readily available in health shops and Greek shops. Easy to make with a food processor, it is so good to eat with fresh Pitta Bread (page 86). You can serve it on its own or as part of a *mezze* (mixed hors d'oeuvre). You can vary the quantity of chick peas you use (or not use any in which case it becomes tahina dip) or change the recipe by using yogurt in place of the oil if you wish. *Serves 4–6.*

100 g (4 oz) uncooked chick peas,
    soaked overnight or 200 g
    (7 oz) cooked or canned
2–3 cloves garlic, skinned
150 ml ($\frac{1}{4}$ pint) tahina paste
4–5 ml ($\frac{3}{4}$–1 tsp) salt
100 ml (4 fl oz) fresh lemon juice
150 ml ($\frac{1}{4}$ pint) olive oil

TO GARNISH
parsley
paprika (optional)
cumin (optional)

If using uncooked chick peas, drain them and cover generously with fresh water. Simmer for 1–2 hours until tender. Drain the chick peas, reserving the cooking liquid. If you like a very smooth dip you can squeeze each pea from its skin or pass the mixture through a sieve.

USING THE METAL BLADE: process the chick peas and garlic until very finely chopped. Add the tahina and salt and process again, gradually trickling in lemon juice, oil and the reserved chick pea water alternately until you arrive at a creamy mixture which will just drop off a spoon. Adjust the seasoning and turn into a bowl. Garnish with parsley or sprinkle with paprika or cumin and serve with warm Pitta Bread (page 86).

GOAT CHEESE, SPINACH AND PINE NUT ROULADE

Slices of this roulade are rather nice arranged attractively on a plate and served as a first course, sprinkled with a little cold-pressed or other good quality olive oil and lemon juice. *Serves 4–6.*

225 g (8 oz) fresh spinach
45 ml (3 tbsp) pine nuts
175 g (6 oz) goat's cheese
30–45 ml (2–3 tbsp) whipping
    cream (if necessary)
pepper
salt (if necessary)

TO SERVE
a few salad leaves
olive oil
$\frac{1}{2}$–1 lemon
freshly ground black pepper

Blanch enough spinach leaves to cover a 20 × 30 cm (8 × 12 inch) area; refresh under the cold tap and pat dry carefully on absorbent kitchen paper. Cook the remaining spinach, refresh and drain well; squeeze out any excess moisture with your hands. Dry fry the pine nuts in a heavy frying pan over a moderate heat, tossing around until they are evenly browned. Remove any rind or bloom from the cheese.

USING THE METAL BLADE: process the spinach until smooth then add in the cheese and pepper, salt if the cheese isn't too salty and process until completely smooth. Thin with a little cream if necessary but keep the mixture stiff so it holds its shape. Finally, toss in the roasted pine nuts and process just to mix in without chopping up finely.

Lay the blanched leaves out on a piece of cling film; form the cheese and spinach mixture into a roll down the middle of the leaves and carefully roll up into a 4 cm (1$\frac{1}{2}$ inch) diameter cylinder. Chill then serve as a log or slice thinly, arranging 4–5 slices like the petals of a flower on a plate and decorate with a few salad leaves. When ready to serve, sprinkle with very best olive oil, a little lemon juice and freshly ground black pepper. Hand crisp hot toast with this dish.

MOUAMARA (SPICED NUT SPREAD AND DIP)

This is rather fun. I got the idea from an old Cypriot book which gives very little indication of quantities, just calling it 'a very spicy spread' and mentioning 1½ tbsp of cayenne and about ¼ lb of cumin! I have been much more circumspect and I have also discovered that it makes a delicious dip if thinned with oil, water and lemon juice and parsley is added. The paste is like a sophisticated and spicy peanut butter, the dip like a tahina variation. *Makes about 375 g (12 oz) jar and serves 4–6.*

THE SPREAD
20 ml (4 tsp) cumin seeds
50 g (2 oz) brown bread
1 shallot or ½ small onion,
 skinned and cut up
50 g (2 oz) salted peanuts
50 g (2 oz) walnuts
2.5 ml (½ tsp) ground cinnamon
1–2.5 ml (¼–½ tsp) cayenne
2.5–5 ml (½–1 tsp) salt (optional)
50 ml (2 fl oz) oil

THE DIP
The Spread ingredients plus:
very large handful parsley heads
juice of about 1 lemon
50–100 ml (2–4 fl oz) oil
salt (optional)

To make the spread: roast the cumin seed in a heavy dry pan over a moderate heat until fragrant and browning; then crush in a pestle and mortar.

USING THE METAL BLADE: break in the bread and add the roughly cut up onion to the bowl. Process to crumbs. Add the nuts, ground spices and salt, if using, and process until the nuts are finely chopped then trickle in the oil and 50 ml (2 fl oz) of water. Do not process too smooth. Pack into a pot and serve spread on biscuits or bread. You can pack some into a pot and turn the rest into the dip if you want. Quantities are not crucial so just add till it tastes nice to you.

To make the dip: if making from scratch, add the parsley in to chop with the nuts but if continuing, having made the spread, add the parsley heads to the bowl. Process until smooth then, with the machine running, gradually add the lemon juice, then the oil and a little water to make a soft dropping consistency. Taste and add salt if necessary. Turn into a shallow bowl and serve with crudités and Pitta Bread (page 86).

CLAM AND SAFFRON DIP

Dips for dunking vegetables, crisps or little biscuits are always popular. This dip is made from curd cheese and a little can of clams and is flavoured with saffron and chives; it can also be used as a dressing for a pasta salad or served with any green salad. If you want a thicker mixture or the clam juice in the can seems rather copious, reduce it before soaking the saffron. *Serves 6–8 as a dip, 4–6 as a first course.*

100 g (4 oz) can clams in juice
1 packet saffron or pinch of
 saffron threads
200 g (7 oz) full or medium fat
 curd cheese
1 clove garlic, skinned
shake Tabasco
salt
pepper
plenty of fresh chives
squeeze lemon juice, to taste

Strain the clam juice into a pan and heat it up; add the saffron and let it soak for 10–15 minutes.

USING THE METAL BLADE: process the cheese with the drained clams, garlic, Tabasco and salt and pepper. Once smooth, trickle in the cooled saffron liquid, snip in the chives and add lemon juice to taste. Do not overprocess cream cheese as it can curdle.

Turn into a bowl and serve surrounded by crudités.

SAVOURY AND SWEET MOUSSES AND SOUFFLÉS

Mousses and soufflés were once time-consuming creations, the preserves of the master chef. Not so now: with the processor you can magic them up in no time at all. With just a small amount of an exotic ingredient you can, with the help of your machine, transform a basic mousse or soufflé mixture into a spectacular party piece. For those who are worried by soufflés sinking on them as they wait for guests, how about the Twice Cooked Cauliflower Soufflé with Cheese Sauce (page 24)? You make it, reheat it and it is delicious.

HOT FISH TURBAN (FISKEFARSE)

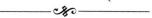

Absolutely top quality fresh fish is essential for this delicate Norwegian dish which is quite wonderful when made with a food processor. The mixture can either be cooked in a ring mould, poached as quenelles or made into little fish balls and served in soup. You can serve it plain or with a delicate parsley or shrimp sauce, accompanied by boiled potatoes. *Serves 4–6.*

350 g (¾ lb) very fresh haddock or
    cod fillet, skinned
75 g (3 oz) very soft butter
2 eggs
15 ml (1 tbsp) potato flour
5 ml (1 tsp) salt
a little pepper
300 ml (½ pint) creamy milk
    or milk and cream mixed

USING THE METAL BLADE: carefully remove all the bones from the fish. Cut into pieces and process until smooth; then add the very soft butter (if it's not soft, it will not combine evenly and will give a curdled consistency). Once the butter is processed in, add the eggs, one at a time, then the potato flour and salt and pepper. Now gradually add the milk as the machine runs until you have a firm, lithe mixture.

Turn into a well-greased 1.2 litre (2 pint) ring mould and set in a bain-marie of hot water. Cook in a warm oven 170°C (325°F) mark 3 for 30–40 minutes until the mixture has just set. Leave for 5 minutes to make turning out easier; run a knife point round both rims and turn out onto a serving dish. Best served at once.

NOTE: these sorts of mixtures are very inclined to work their way into the centre column of the blade which then needs to be thoroughly cleaned.

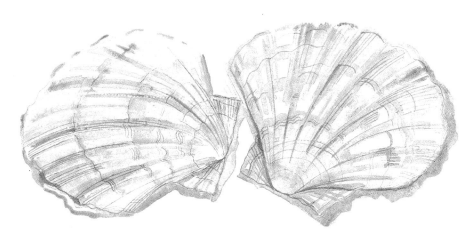

QUENELLES WITH PRAWN MOUSSELINE

The elegant quenelle, once the preserve of great restaurants, has now, thanks to the food processor, come within everyone's grasp. These quenelles are made from fresh whiting and are flavoured with prawns. The prawn shells are pulverised in the food processor to enhance the taste of the mousseline sauce. *Serves 4–6.*

---

350 g (12 oz) prawns, unshelled
250 g (9 oz) fillet of whiting,
   trimmed and skinned
3 egg whites
salt
pepper
mace
350 ml (12 fl oz) double cream

PRAWN MOUSSELINE
150 g (5½ oz) unsalted or lightly
   salted butter
prawn shells
300 ml (½ pint) fish fumet or
   ½ fish stock cube and water
2 egg yolks
½–1 lemon
salt
pepper

Set 6–8 prawns aside for garnish. Shell the rest, reserving the shells for the mousseline. Prepare the sauce base while the quenelle mixture rests.

USING THE METAL BLADE: make the quenelle mixture. Pick over the whiting, removing all bones. Process the fish with the prawns until finely chopped, adding the egg whites and, when absolutely smooth, season lightly with salt, pepper and a tiny bit of mace. If the mixture isn't quite smooth, sieve it. With the machine running, add the cream quickly but do not process for more than 20 seconds or the mixture might curdle. The mixture must be firm enough to sit up on a spoon. Chill for 30 minutes or so before cooking.

Bring a wide, shallow pan of salted water to the simmer. Dip a dessertspoon in warm water and take a good rounded spoonful of the quenelle mixture; shape if necessary with another wet spoon and lower into the water (tap the spoon on the bottom until the quenelle detaches). Form all the quenelles and poach for about 8–10 minutes, carefully turning once with a slotted spoon, until just firm. Remove with a slotted spoon, drain on absorbent kitchen paper and keep warm, well covered and spaced a little apart in a buttered shallow serving dish. Put the reserved prawns to heat as well.

To make the prawn mousseline: melt 75 g (3 oz) of the butter in a frying pan, add the reserved prawn shells and toss over the heat for 1 minute until heated through.

USING THE METAL BLADE: scrape the prawn-shell mixture into the bowl and process until well chopped; then turn into a sieve, lined with a generous piece of muslin, and wring out all the prawn butter. Cool.

Place the prawn shells in a saucepan with the fish fumet or stock cube and water and simmer for 10 minutes, skimming if any scum forms. Strain through muslin then reduce the prawn fumet until strongly flavoured and only 75 ml (3 fl oz) remains.

USING THE METAL BLADE: pour the hot prawn fumet into the bowl and process whilst adding dice of the remaining butter and prawn butter. Once it is all emulsified, turn it into a small pan and set aside until ready to serve.

Place the egg yolks with 10 ml (2 tsp) of lemon juice and 30 ml (2 tbsp) of cold water in a bowl over hot water. Cook, whisking all the time, until the mixture doubles in bulk, becomes moussey and just holds a trail. Reboil the butter mixture and gradually whisk it into the egg mousseline. Continue whisking over hot water until it is a light coating consistency; adjust the seasoning and add lemon juice to taste. The sauce can be kept warm over tepid water.

To serve the dish: spoon the sauce over the quenelles and decorate with the heated unpeeled prawns. Serve at once.

TOMATO MOUSSE WITH SEAFOOD AND BASIL SAUCE

An all year round mousse, which evokes summer days with its tomato and basil flavouring. It makes a useful summer lunch dish or a starter for supper parties. You can vary it by using curd cheese instead of cream cheese, yogurt or soured cream instead of cream or mayonnaise in place of either. For a lighter mousse, you can whip the cream at the end and fold it into the mixture as it begins to set. The sauce can be accented in different ways with various herbs and can be lightened by substituting yogurt for the cream. You can also add cubes of poached, drained monkfish to make this a more substantial dish. *Serves 4–6.*

15 ml (1 tbsp) gelatine
60 ml (4 tbsp) vermouth
400 g (15 oz) can peeled plum
 tomatoes
½ shallot or bit of spring onion
6–8 fresh basil leaves or 2.5 ml
 (½ tsp) dried
100 g (4 oz) full fat cream cheese
salt
pepper
150 ml (¼ pint) whipping cream

SEAFOOD SAUCE
200–300 g (7–11 oz) prawns,
 unshelled
150 ml (¼ pint) dry white wine
sprig thyme
1 clove garlic, peeled
150 ml (¼ pint) thick mayonnaise
6–8 fresh basil leaves or 2.5 ml
 (½ tsp) dried
salt
pepper
lemon juice or vinegar, to taste
50–75 ml (2–3 fl oz) whipping
 cream

TO GARNISH
watercress or salad leaves

Sprinkle the gelatine onto the vermouth in a small bowl and set aside for a few minutes to soak; then stand the bowl in a pan of hot water to melt the gelatine. Drain the can of tomatoes over a sieve and reserve the liquid.

USING THE METAL BLADE: place the drained tomatoes in the food processor with the shallot or spring onion and basil and process until smooth; then, with the machine running, add the reserved tomato liquid. Strain through a sieve to remove the pips and set aside. Place the cream cheese in the bowl, process briefly until smooth then gradually add the sieved tomato mixture, processing until smooth; then season with salt and pepper, add the gelatine and finally the cream. Be careful not to over-process. Pour into an oiled 1.1 litre (2 pint) ring mould and leave to set in a cool, level place.

To make the seafood sauce: shell the prawns, reserving the shells.

USING THE METAL BLADE: chop the prawn shells roughly with the on/off or pulse technique. Turn the shells into a pan with 150 ml (¼ pint) of water, the wine, thyme and garlic. Boil hard for about 10 minutes then strain off the liquid through muslin, squeezing the debris well: Discard the prawn shells. Boil down the prawn liquid until only 30–45 ml (2–3 tbsp) of syrupy liquid remains. Cool.

USING THE METAL BLADE: process the mayonnaise, basil, salt, pepper and a good squeeze of lemon juice then add the prawn liquid and cream to make a light sauce. Adjust the seasoning and stir in the prawns. Turn into a sauceboat.

To serve the mousse: dip the mould in hot water for a moment, dry and unmould onto a serving dish. Fill the centre with watercress or a green salad and serve the sauce separately.

Twice Cooked Cauliflower Soufflé with Cheese Sauce

Twice cooked soufflés can be prepared at your leisure and reheated to bubbling brown succulence whenever you like. You can vary the base by using broccoli, courgette or crab and the coating sauce by flavouring it with curry or tomato. It's also a very good way of turning leftovers into something exciting. Instead of making it in a ring mould you could use individual cocotte dishes. *Serves 4–6.*

40 g (1½ oz) butter
40 g (1½ oz) plain flour
200–225 ml (7–8 fl oz) milk
salt
pepper
nutmeg
225 g (8 oz) cooked cauliflower
 or calabrese
4 egg yolks
5 egg whites

CHEESE SAUCE
75–100 g (3–4 oz) grated Gruyère
 cheese or Cheddar cheese
25 g (1 oz) butter
25 g (1 oz) plain flour
300 ml (½ pint) milk
75 ml (3 fl oz) whipping cream
salt
pepper

To make the soufflé: melt the butter, add the flour and cook, stirring, over a moderate heat for 1–2 minutes. Draw off the stove, wait for it to stop sizzling and then add the milk. Bring to the boil, whisking hard, season with salt, pepper and nutmeg and simmer for 2–3 minutes.

USING THE METAL BLADE: process the cauliflower to a purée then add the thick sauce and, one at a time, the yolks. Turn the mixture into a bowl.

USING THE EGG WHISK OR A HAND WHISK AND A VERY CLEAN BOWL: whip up the whites until just holding a peak. Fold a spoonful carefully into the cauliflower mixture to lighten it, then gently fold in the remaining whites. Turn the mixture into an extremely well greased 1.7 litre (3 pint) ring mould and cook in a bain-marie in a moderately hot oven 190°C (375°F) mark 5 for 10–15 minutes until just firm and set. Leave to cool for at least 20 minutes or up to 24 hours if you wish. Turn out the cauliflower soufflé (which will by now be very shrunk and wrinkled looking, but don't worry) on to a greased ovenproof dish.

USING THE STANDARD GRATER: make the cheese sauce. Grate the cheese and set it aside. Melt the butter, add the flour and cook gently, stirring, over a moderate heat for 1–2 minutes. Draw off the stove, wait for it to stop sizzling and then add the milk and cream and bring to the boil while whisking hard. Simmer for 2–3 minutes, then season with salt and pepper and stir in the cheese.

USING THE METAL BLADE: turn into the food processor and process until smooth and velvety. Spoon over the soufflé.

Rebake the soufflé in a fairly hot oven 200°C (400°F) mark 6 for about 10–15 minutes until it is puffed up, heated through and the sauce is just bubbling. Serve at once.

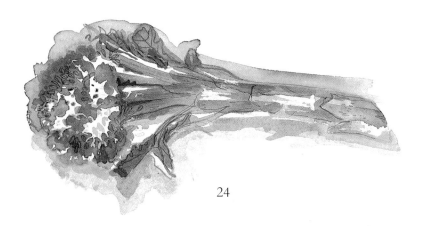

CRAB MOUSSE WITH DILL

This is a delightful summer mousse made with fresh crab, dill and cream cheese. It is very quick and easy to prepare. *Serves 4–6.*

10 ml (2 tsp) gelatine
250 g (9 oz) cooked crab meat,
    brown and white
small bunch dill
175 g (6 oz) full fat cream cheese
salt
pepper
$\frac{1}{8}$ tsp mace
150 ml ($\frac{1}{4}$ pint) yogurt
2 egg whites
good squeeze lemon juice

TO GARNISH
crab claws (optional)
sliced cucumber

Place 30 ml (2 tbsp) of cold water in a bowl, sprinkle in the gelatine and leave to soak for a few minutes. Stand the bowl in a pan of hot water to dissolve the gelatine.

USING THE METAL BLADE: place the crab meat and tender dill sprigs in the bowl; process to chop and mix. Add the cream cheese and season with salt, pepper and mace. Process briefly with the on/off or pulse technique, stirring down if necessary, until smooth then add the yogurt. Add the cooled, dissolved gelatine, and the lemon juice and process to combine.

USING THE EGG WHISK OR A HAND WHISK AND VERY CLEAN BOWL: whisk the egg whites until just holding a peak and carefully fold into the mixture. Turn into a 600 ml (1 pint) soufflé dish and chill until set. Garnish with crab claws and thinly sliced cucumber.

LEMON CURD MOUSSE

This is a wonderfully useful and quick pudding; a creamless lemon mousse. Gelatine is easy to use with a food processor but, if you prefer, you can leave it out and eat the pudding as a lemon curd foam if you serve it within an hour or so of making it—before it collapses. If you do this, serve it in individual glasses. *Serves 4–6.*

7 ml ($1\frac{1}{2}$ tsp) gelatine
3 eggs, separated
100 g (4 oz) caster sugar
the grated rind and juice from
    $1\frac{1}{2}$ large or 2 small lemons
60 g ($2\frac{1}{2}$ oz) butter

Put 30 ml (2 tbsp) of cold water in a bowl and sprinkle on the gelatine. Leave to soak to form a jellied cake.

USING THE METAL BLADE: place the egg yolks and all but 30 ml (2 tbsp) of the sugar in the food processor; process for about 1 minute until thick and pale. Place the lemon juice, rind and butter in a small saucepan and heat just to boiling point.

Add the soaked gelatine cake, process and immediately pour the hot lemon-butter mixture down the feed tube; process for a further $\frac{1}{2}$–1 minute to ensure the gelatine is melted and to thicken the mixture.

USING THE WHISK ATTACHMENT OR A HAND WHISK AND A VERY CLEAN BOWL: whip the egg whites until they just hold a peak; whisk in the reserved sugar then fold in the hot lemon mixture. Turn into a 600 ml (1 pint) soufflé dish or glass bowl. Chill for 4–6 hours, before serving.

THE MOST CHOCOLATY MOUSSE

Nearly everybody loves a chocolate mousse from time to time, the more chocolaty the better; this one is light but very chocolaty. The secret is that you must use good chocolate; I use Lindt Excellence for this but Chocolate Meunier or Terry's Plain are also good. I like to make it absolutely plain with just chocolate but you can vary it by adding liqueur or some grated orange rind or you can substitute orange juice for the water. *Serves 4–6.*

175 g (6 oz) best dark chocolate
25 g (1 oz) unsalted or lightly
  salted butter
2–3 drops vanilla essence
  (optional)
30 ml (2 tbsp) brandy, orange
  liqueur, Crème de Cacao or
  Tia Maria (optional)
3 eggs, separated
150 ml (¼ pint) whipping cream
30 ml (2 tbsp) caster sugar

Break up the chocolate and set it to melt with the butter, 45 ml (3 tbsp) of water, vanilla and brandy (if using) in a bowl over hot water; then leave to cool a little.

USING THE METAL BLADE: process the egg yolks for about 30 seconds until a pale yellow colour; scrape in the softened chocolate mixture and process together for about 1 minute. Once the mixture is cool and the chocolate starts to thicken, pour the cream down the feed tube and process for 20–40 seconds until the mixture thickens. Don't overprocess or the cream may turn to butter.

USING THE EGG WHISK OR A HAND WHISK AND A VERY CLEAN BOWL: Whip the egg whites until just holding a peak, whisk in the sugar until fairly stiff then gently fold into the chocolate mixture. Turn into a 600 ml (1 pint) soufflé dish, glass bowl or individual dishes and leave to set in the fridge for 4–6 hours.

GOOSEBERRY AND SOFT CHEESE MOUSSE

Quark, a soft curd cheese, comes from Germany and fromage blanc from France; now you can get them both here. I like to use one or other of them in this gooseberry mousse which is light and fresh and not too rich. You can adapt this recipe for a number of other soft fruits. *Serves 4–6.*

500 g (1 lb 2 oz) gooseberries
100–175 g (4–6 oz) sugar
2–3 heads elderflower or rose
  geranium leaves (optional)
15 ml (1 tbsp) gelatine
100 g (4 oz) quark, fromage blanc
  or soft curd cheese
150 ml (¼ pint) whipping cream
3 egg whites

Put the gooseberries in a saucepan with the sugar and about 30 ml (2 tbsp) of water, adding elderflower or rose geranium leaves if desired. Cook, covered, until the gooseberries are soft. Remove and discard the flowers. Place 30 ml (2 tbsp) of cold water in a bowl and sprinkle in the gelatine. Leave the gelatine to soak and form a jellied cake.

USING THE METAL BLADE: pour the hot gooseberries into the bowl, add the gelatine cake and process until smooth. Sieve and leave until cool and just beginning to thicken.

USING THE METAL BLADE: process the quark, add the gooseberry purée and then the cream. Process until the cream thickens but do not overprocess or the mixture may curdle.

USING THE EGG WHISK OR A HAND WHISK AND A VERY CLEAN BOWL: whisk the eggs until they just hold a peak, then fold into the gooseberry mixture. Turn into a 900 ml (1½ pint) serving dish and leave to set for 4–6 hours in the fridge before serving.

CREAMED RICE MOUSSE WITH CARAMEL PEACH SAUCE

A nursery-type pudding treated in rather an elegant way to make a very light, creamed rice cake. It appeals to grown ups and children alike. Serve with a fresh fruit purée, such as strawberry, raspberry or mango for a change, or with this caramel flavoured fruit sauce. The sauce can also be made from nectarines or canned apricots. *Serves 6–8.*

100 g (4 oz) round grain
   pudding rice
600 ml (1 pint) milk
75 g (3 oz) vanilla sugar
pinch salt (optional)
15 ml (1 tbsp) gelatine
200 ml (7 fl oz) whipping cream
2 egg whites
2.5 ml ($\frac{1}{2}$ tsp) natural vanilla
   essence

CARAMEL PEACH SAUCE
5–6 fresh peaches or 400 g (14 oz)
   can peaches
100 g (4 oz) caster sugar
   (optional)
75 g (3 oz) caster sugar
15–30 ml (1–2 tbsp) peach or
   apricot brandy (optional)

Sprinkle the rice into a saucepan of cold water and bring just to the boil; then drain. Put the rice back in the pan, add the milk, vanilla sugar and salt to the rice and bring to the boil quickly; stir once then simmer gently, half covered, stirring from time to time for about 30–40 minutes until the rice is very soft and the milk has almost all been absorbed.

Place 30 ml (2 tbsp) of cold water in a cup and sprinkle in the gelatine. Leave for a few minutes until it forms a jellied cake. Stir this into the hot rice until dissolved. Add the vanilla essence and leave until cold and just setting.

USING THE WHISK, PLASTIC OR METAL BLADE: process the cream until it thickens, stopping frequently to check its consistency. If over-processed, it will curdle. Then add the rice mixture in a ring around the bowl and process briefly until mixed. Whisk the egg whites, either using the well washed whisk and a very clean processor bowl or with a hand whisk, and fold into the mixture. Rinse out a 1.2 litre (2 pint) soufflé dish in cold water and turn the mixture into it. Leave to set in the fridge for 4–6 hours.

To make the caramel peach sauce: if using fresh peaches, peel them. Make a sugar syrup with 100 g (4 oz) of caster sugar and 150 ml ($\frac{1}{4}$ pint) of water and poach the fruit in it. Using a slotted spoon, take out the fruit and reserve the fruit and juice separately. Alternatively, drain the can of peaches, reserving the juice. Pour half the reserved peach juice into a saucepan add the 75 g (3 oz) of caster sugar and heat gently, stirring, until the sugar has completely dissolved; then boil fast, without stirring, until the syrup becomes a golden caramel colour. If using canned juice, heat it. Draw the pan of syrup just off the flame and add the remaining hot peach juice as fast as possible. Return to the stove and boil until all the caramel has dissolved and you have a very heavy syrup.

USING THE METAL BLADE: set several peach halves aside for decoration and slice into segments. Process the remainder and once smooth, add in the caramel syrup and if you wish, peach brandy.

TO SERVE: turn the rice mould out onto a serving dish, pour the peach sauce around it and decorate the top with the reserved peach segments. Serve chilled.

SAVOURY AND SWEET PANCAKES AND BATTERS

Pancakes and batters can be made with a never-ending variety of flours and flavourings. You can wrap up parcels of exotic ingredients, make the most of leftovers or layer up vegetables into pies as in Artichoke and Broccoli Pancake Pie (page 31). By varying the ingredients and thickness of batters you can have dishes as light and elegant as Japanese tempura, as delicate as Mixed Vegetable Bhaji (page 33) or as satisfying as Koftas in Herb Batter (page 34). Sweet pancakes and butters also span the range from elegant dinner party dishes like Luxury Praline Filled Pancakes to homely but delicious puddings such as Tutti-Frutti Clafoutis (both on page 36).

SPICED YOGURT PANCAKES WITH GRATED VEGETABLES

These thick but tender pancakes, which have grated vegetables incorporated in the batter can also be made plain; just omit the ginger, onion and spices. They are nice filled with a simple tomato sauce, like the one used in the Speedy Pizza (page 66), but with plenty of onions added. The onions are halved, thickly sliced and gently fried.

Alternatively, you could top them with Kheema with Lettuce (page 42) and hand round cucumber and yogurt salad or Roasted Pepper and Aubergine Dip (page 18). *Serves 4–6.*

½ small onion
handful parsley heads
1–2.5 ml (¼–½ tsp) cayenne
a little fresh root ginger, grated
5 ml (1 tsp) nigella seeds, *kalonji*
2.5 ml (½ tsp) turmeric
2.5 ml (½ tsp) curry powder
2 eggs
225 ml (8 fl oz) yogurt
50 g (2 oz) wholemeal flour or
    granary flour
50 g (2 oz) plain flour
2.5 ml (½ tsp) baking powder
30 ml (2 tbsp) oil
4–5 ml (¾–1 tsp) salt
100 g (4 oz) mixed raw vegetables
    like carrot, celery, onion, raw
    Jerusalem artichoke, turnip,
    radish or parsnip.

USING THE METAL BLADE: make the pancake batter. Roughly chop the onion and parsley with the on/off or pulse technique, then add the spices, eggs, half the yogurt, the flours, baking powder, oil and salt to the processor bowl and process until smooth. Then with the motor running pour in the remaining yogurt. Only grate the vegetables when you are ready to cook the pancakes.

USING THE COARSE GRATING DISC: grate the chosen vegetables into the batter and mix well.

Heat a heavy 18 cm (7 inch) pancake or frying pan and grease with a few drops of oil rubbed on with absorbent kitchen paper. Place about 30 ml (2 tbsp) of the batter in the middle of the pan and shake gently until it spreads to the outer rim. Cook over a moderate heat until the bottom is golden brown and the top just set. Turn with a palette knife and cook the second side until golden. Slip the pancake out of the pan and keep warm between two plates over hot water or in a low oven. Cook the remaining batter in the same way.

Serve plain or with cottage cheese mixed with cream cheese and chives, or in one of the ways suggested above.

CRÊPES FARCIES

These stuffed pancakes can be made with a variety of fresh meats or you can adapt the recipe to use leftover roast meat. The sauce is flavoured with the meat gravy, giving it an added richness. It is good served on a bed of spinach leaves. *Serves 4–6.*

7–15 g (¼–½ oz) dried *cèpes* mushrooms or about 200 g (7 oz) fresh mushrooms
300 ml (½ pint) stock
1 large onion, quartered
50 g (2 oz) butter or vegetable oil
100–200 g (4–7 oz) smoked bacon, diced
2 carrots, cut up
1 stick celery
500–700 g (1 lb 2 oz–1½ lb) lean pork, beef, lamb or chicken, diced
45–60 ml (3–4 tbsp) marsala, sherry or wine
45–60 ml (3–4 tbsp) tomato purée
salt
pepper
nutmeg
1 egg, beaten

PANCAKES—MAKES 10–12
1 egg
1 egg yolk
100 g (4 oz) plain flour
2.5 ml (½ tsp) salt
100 ml (4 fl oz) milk
30 ml (2 tbsp) vegetable oil
vegetable oil, for greasing

SAUCE
25 g (1 oz) butter
25 g (1 oz) plain flour
300 ml (½ pint) milk
salt
pepper

TO GARNISH
75 g (3 oz) Gruyère or Cheddar cheese, grated

If you are using dried *cèpes*, soak them in hot stock for about 30 minutes.

USING THE METAL BLADE: chop the onion roughly with the on/off or pulse technique. Do not over-process it to a wet or pulpy state. Heat the butter or oil in a large frying pan or sauté pan and brown the onions in it; add the bacon. Roughly chop the carrot with the on/off or pulse technique and add it to the pan; then chop the celery and add it as well. Fry the vegetables and bacon for a good 10–15 minutes until a good golden brown.

USING THE METAL BLADE: drop the meat onto the moving blades in small batches; stop and remove once minced. Add the meat to the pan of vegetables and fry until it is golden brown. Drain the *cèpes*, reserving the stock. Dice the dried *cèpes* and add them.

USING THE MEDIUM SLICING DISC: slice the fresh mushrooms, if using, add to the pan and fry. Once the meat is well browned, add the marsala and boil until completely evaporated. Add the tomato purée and fry for 1–2 minutes. Add the reserved stock and stir well; season with salt and pepper and add some freshly grated nutmeg. Cover, or turn into a flameproof casserole, and simmer for about 1 hour, stirring and moistening if necessary, until the meat is cooked and the juices rich and syrupy. Turn into a sieve and reserve the juices. Mix the egg into the meat and adjust the seasoning.

While the meat is cooking, make the pancakes. First make the batter.

USING THE METAL BLADE: place the egg and the yolk in the bowl with the milk, the flour and the salt. Process until smooth, then gradually add 100–150 ml (4–6 fl oz) of water and the oil. Heat a 20 cm (8 inch) pancake pan and grease. Swirl about half a coffee cupful of batter over the base of the pan, pouring back any excess. Cook until brown on one side then turn and brown the other side. Pile on a plate until ready to use. Thin the batter if necessary to achieve fine pancakes.

To make the sauce: melt the butter, add the flour and cook over a moderate heat, stirring, for 1–2 minutes. Draw off the stove, wait for it to stop sizzling and then add the milk and reserved meat juices. Bring to the boil, whisking hard, season with salt and pepper and simmer for 1–2 minutes.

USING THE METAL BLADE: if you want a more velvety texture, process the sauce.

To finish the dish: lay a spoonful of filling across the centre of each pancake and roll it up. Place in one layer in a buttered ovenproof dish. Pour over the sauce and sprinkle with the cheese. Reheat briefly in a fairly hot oven 200°C (400°F) mark 6 and brown under the grill before serving. If reheating from cold, allow 20–30 minutes in the oven for the filling to heat through and the top to brown.

PRAWN AND CUCUMBER KROMESKI

A fresh, light filling of prawn and crunchy cucumber is parcelled in a pancake, rolled in egg and breadcrumbs and fried to make an exquisitely crisp kromeski. You can use the sauce base with all sorts of other ingredients and leftovers like mushrooms, ham, chicken or smoked fish to make your own special fried parcels. They make a lovely first course for entertaining or a special supper dish. *Serves 4–6.*

PANCAKES
2 eggs
150 ml ($\frac{1}{4}$ pint) milk
100 g (4 oz) plain flour
2.5 ml ($\frac{1}{2}$ tsp) salt
75–150 ml (3–5 fl oz) soda water,
    Perrier or water
30 ml (2 tbsp) walnut, olive or
    other flavoured oil
vegetable oil, for greasing

PRAWN AND CUCUMBER
FILLING
$\frac{1}{2}$–$\frac{3}{4}$ cucumber, unpeeled
salt
25 g (1 oz) butter
150 ml ($\frac{1}{4}$ pint) milk
50 g (2 oz) plain flour
1 egg yolk
150 ml ($\frac{1}{4}$ pint) yogurt
225 g (8 oz) peeled prawns
pepper
nutmeg
a little grated lemon rind
a little fresh or dried tarragon
15–30 ml (1–2 tbsp) double cream
    (optional)
1–2 eggs
vegetable oil
dried breadcrumbs, for coating

TO GARNISH
sprigs of tarragon
cucumber slices
peeled prawns

USING THE METAL BLADE: make the pancake batter. Break the eggs into the bowl and add the milk, flour and salt. Process until smooth then gradually add the soda water and oil to make a thin cream-like consistency. Grease a 20 cm (8 inch) crêpe pan and heat. Swirl in about half a coffee cupful of batter over the base of the pan, pouring back any excess. Cook until brown on one side then turn and brown the other side. Make 12 thin pancakes, piling them on a plate when made.

USING THE THICK 6 mm SLICER OR DICE THE CUCUMBER BY HAND: cut the cucumber into lengthways strips to fit the feed tube; pack the tube tightly and slice with medium-firm pressure to make neat small dice. Toss into boiling salted water and blanch for 30 seconds; drain, refresh under cold, running water and drain thoroughly.

To make the sauce: melt the butter.

USING THE METAL BLADE: pour the melted butter and milk into the bowl. Add the flour and egg yolk and process until smooth; add the yogurt, process briefly and turn into a heavy saucepan. Bring just to the boil, whisking until smooth. (Only just boil because longer cooking will bring out a floury flavour that will take some time to cook away. The flour stabilises the yogurt and egg yolk so they do not curdle.) Pat the prawns and cucumber dry with absorbent kitchen paper, add to the pan and season with salt, pepper, nutmeg, a little grated lemon rind and some chopped tarragon. If the mixture is very thick add a little double cream.

Whisk the eggs with a little salt and a few drops of vegetable oil. Divide the mixture between the pancakes. Turn in the two sides, brush with a little egg, roll up the pancake and seal the end with egg. Dip all the pancakes in the egg mixture and roll in breadcrumbs.

Heat the oil in a deep frying pan or wok to 180°C (350°F) and fry several kromeski at a time until crisp and a good brown. Drain on absorbent kitchen paper and keep warm in a moderate oven 180°C (350°F) mark 4 while you fry the remainder. Serve at once, garnished with sprigs of parsley.

See illustration facing page 32

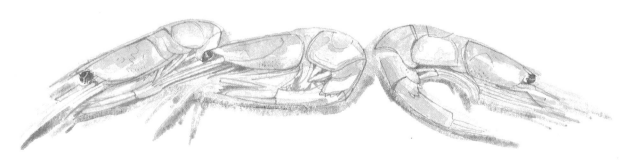

ARTICHOKE AND BROCCOLI PANCAKE PIE

The trouble with layered pancake dishes is that so often the pancakes have gone soft and soggy. To avoid this I have made the pie in a large ring mould (or you could use a cake tin) which is turned out to finish crisping in the oven so the pancakes turn into a crispy golden crust. Use just one vegetable if you wish or start experimenting with other combinations like spinach and carrot, parsnip and mushroom or aubergine and peppers. You can also add a little diced fried smoky bacon for flavour if you don't especially want a vegetarian dish. *Serves 4–6.*

---

1 batch pancakes as for Crêpe Farcies (page 29)

FILLING
450 g (1 lb) Jerusalem artichokes, peeled
25 g (1 oz) butter
salt
pepper
400–450 g (14 oz–1 lb) broccoli
nutmeg
200 g (7 oz) cream or curd cheese
4 eggs
25 g (1 oz) freshly grated Parmesan cheese
150 ml (¼ pint) milk
25 g (1 oz) butter, plus extra, for greasing
1–2 cloves garlic, chopped

TOMATO SAUCE
(page 43) (optional)

Make the pancakes (page 29).

USING THE CHIPPER BLADE: chip the artichokes, using firm pressure on the plunger. Heat the butter in a frying pan and sauté the artichokes for 3–4 minutes until just softening. Season with salt and pepper and set aside. Trim the broccoli, peeling thick stems with a potato peeler and cut into even-sized pieces. Steam until just tender.

USING THE METAL BLADE: process the broccoli until roughly chopped and season with salt, pepper and nutmeg. Set aside.

USING THE METAL BLADE: process the soft cheese, briefly, until smooth; add an egg and process again briefly, stirring down once. Now add the remaining eggs and process for a moment or two to combine before adding the Parmesan cheese and seasoning. With the engine running, pour in the milk. Do not process for longer than about 20 seconds in all or the mixture may curdle.

To assemble the dish: heat the butter with the chopped garlic to make garlic butter; discard the garlic pieces. Paint the inside of a 1.7 litre (3 pint) ring mould or cake tin with butter and line with pancakes, each painted lightly with garlic butter; overlap the pancakes to make a double thickness with the edges hanging over the rim. Spoon the artichoke into the pancake-lined tin and pour over half the cheese and egg mixture; cover with a layer of pancakes, brush with garlic butter, again with the edges hanging over the rim. Now fill the mould with the chopped broccoli and pour over the remaining cheese and egg mixture. Brush the remaining pancakes with garlic butter (fold in half for the ring mould) and cover the top of the mould before turning in the pancakes hanging over the edges. Place, uncovered, in a fairly hot oven 200°C (400°F) mark 6 for about 30–35 minutes until the filling has set. Remove from the oven and leave to stand for about 5 minutes so it will turn out more easily; then run a knife round the rim and turn out on to an ovenproof serving plate. Return to the hot oven for about 5–10 minutes for the pancakes to become crisp and golden then serve at once, cut in wedges like a cake. Hand round Tomato Sauce, if you wish.

BUCKWHEAT PANCAKES
WITH BLUE CHEESE FONDUTA

Buckwheat is traditionally used in Bretonne pancakes. Here I have used it to make interesting pancakes which I like to serve with Cambazola sauce and plenty of chopped chives. They are also nice filled with spinach or stir-fried vegetables and served, coated with the Blue Cheese Fonduta. You can also use these pancakes for sweet dishes. *Serves 4–6.*

BUCKWHEAT PANCAKES

2 eggs

300 ml ($\frac{1}{2}$ pint) mixed milk and water

50 g (2 oz) buckwheat flour

50 g (2 oz) plain flour

30 ml (2 tbsp) wheatgerm (optional)

2.5 ml ($\frac{1}{2}$ tsp) salt

30 ml (2 tbsp) vegetable oil plus vegetable oil for frying

BLUE CHEESE FONDUTA

50 ml (2 fl oz) milk

25 g (1 oz) butter

100 g (4 oz) Cambazola or other soft blue cheese, derinded

2.5 ml ($\frac{1}{2}$ tsp) potato flour or cornflour

1 egg yolk

a few drops Worcestershire sauce

salt

pepper

cayenne

TO FINISH

plenty of chopped chives or lemon thyme

USING THE METAL BLADE: make the pancake batter. Break the eggs into the bowl, add half the liquid, the flours, wheatgerm and salt; process until smooth. With the engine running, add the remaining liquid and the oil down the feed tube. Add a little more water if necessary to make batter the consistency of thin cream.

Grease a 20 cm (8 inch) pan and heat. Pour in a little batter; swirl around the pan and cook until brown on one side; turn over carefully and cook the second side. Pile on a plate, cover and keep warm over steam or in a low oven.

To make the Blue Cheese Fonduta: heat the milk and butter in a saucepan until the butter has melted.

USING THE METAL BLADE: break the cheese up into the bowl and add the potato flour and yolk; process and gradually add the warm liquid, stopping to stir down if necessary, until you have a smooth mixture; then add the Worcestershire sauce, salt, pepper and cayenne. Process and turn into a heavy pan. Heat gently, stirring, until the sauce is hot and has thickened. Do not boil.

To serve: spread each pancake with a little sauce and some chopped chives, fold in quarters and serve at once.

Prawn and cucumber kromeski (page 30)

Overleaf: Indonesian saté with yellow rice and creamy peanut sauce (page 41)

FISH FILLETS IN CRISPY BEER BATTER

This batter, made with beer and yeast is very light and crisp. You can use it to coat fresh fish fillets or strips of sole. Well fried and served with Sauce Gribiche (page 75) or Parsley Sauce (page 76), it is a treat. This is a versatile batter that can be used to make fritters from apples, bananas, courgettes, aubergines or sorrel leaves. If you don't have any yeast to hand, make the batter without it and leave it in a warm place for about 4 hours to ferment. *Serves 4–6.*

BATTER
125 g (5 oz) plain flour
2.5 ml ($\frac{1}{2}$ tsp) salt
5 ml (1 tsp) fresh yeast
75 ml (3 fl oz) beer
15 ml (1 tbsp) vegetable oil
vegetable oil, for deep frying
**4–6 × 100–175 g (4–6 oz) fillets of
    fresh haddock or cod, skinned**

TO SERVE
lemon wedges
**Sauce Gribiche (page 75) or
    Parsley Sauce (page 76)**

USING THE METAL BLADE: make the batter. Place the flour, salt and yeast in the bowl. Process and, with the engine running, add the beer, 75 ml (3 fl oz) of tepid water and the oil to make a smooth batter which should coat the back of a spoon. Leave to ferment in a warm place for 30–40 minutes.

Heat the oil in a deep fryer to 185°C (360°F). Stir up the batter to expel any air bubbles, dip the skinned fish into the batter, drain for a moment then lower into the hot oil. Fry for about 2–3 minutes, depending on the thickness of the fillet, until a good golden brown. Drain on absorbent kitchen paper and serve at once with lemon wedges and Sauce Gribiche (page 75) or Parsley Sauce (page 76).

MIXED VEGETABLE BHAJI

These spicy, deep-fried lacy Indian fritters can be served crisp and hot as an appetiser with drinks or as an accompaniment to an Indian meal. Chickpea flour is available in health shops and from Indian stores, where it is known as *gram* or *besan* flour. Black cumin seeds are also sold there. You can make these using sifted wholemeal flour, in which case you will need to adjust the amount of liquid used. *Serves 6–8 as an appetiser, 4–6 as a main course.*

**100 g (4 oz) chickpea or
    wholemeal flour**
5 ml (1 tsp) salt
good pinch bicarbonate of soda
2.5 ml ($\frac{1}{2}$ tsp) ground turmeric
**5 ml (1 tsp) whole black cumin
    seeds**
5–15 ml (1–3) tsp) curry powder
$\frac{1}{8}$–$\frac{1}{4}$ tsp chilli or cayenne
**500 g (1 lb 2 oz) mixture of raw
    vegetables, eg: onion, carrot,
    celeriac, turnip, potato, pepper
    or green beans**
vegetable oil, for deep frying

USING THE METAL BLADE: sift the flour, salt and bicarbonate of soda into the bowl; add the turmeric, cumin, curry powder and chilli. Switch on and gradually add 150–175 ml (5–6 fl oz) of water to make a creamy batter.

USING THE COARSE GRATING DISC: grate the vegetables into the batter. Turn it all into a bowl and stir.

Heat some oil in a deep fat fryer or a wok and when hot 185°C (360°F) and just hazing, fry small spoonfuls of the mixture, a few at a time, to make lacy golden-brown vegetable fritters. Drain on absorbent kitchen paper and hand round piping hot.

KOFTAS IN HERB BATTER

This batter, without the onion, parsley and spices, is the one I use for toad-in-the-hole. Here, perked up a bit, it is cooked with large-sized Lamb Koftas (page 43) in it instead of sausages. *Serves 4–6.*

BATTER
2 eggs
1 small onion, roughly cut up
handful of parsley heads
2.5 ml ($\frac{1}{2}$ tsp) cumin seeds
2.5 ml ($\frac{1}{2}$ tsp) turmeric
300 ml ($\frac{1}{2}$ pint) milk
175 g (6 oz) plain flour
2.5 ml ($\frac{1}{2}$ tsp) salt
pepper
1–1$\frac{1}{2}$ batches Lamb Kofta mixture (page 43)
60–90 ml (4–6 tbsp) vegetable oil

USING THE METAL BLADE: make the batter. Break the eggs into the food processor bowl, add the onion and the parsley heads, the cumin seeds, turmeric, the milk, flour and salt and pepper. Process until smooth; then add up to 150 ml ($\frac{1}{4}$ pint) of cold water to make a pouring consistency.

Make up 1–1$\frac{1}{2}$ times the Kofta mixture (page 43) and form into 12–18 balls. Heat the oil in a frying pan or wok and fry the balls briefly until lightly brown; set aside. Pour oil into a 25 × 30 cm (10 × 12 inch) roasting pan just to coat it and place in a hot oven 220°C (425°F) mark 7 until the fat is smoking. Pour the batter in and arrange the koftas on it. Return to the oven and cook for 35–45 minutes, until the batter is well risen and golden brown. Serve at once.

PRAWN AND VEGETABLE TEMPURA

The light and delicate batter used by the Japanese to coat food for deep frying can be whisked up in a food processor in no time. This quantity will serve two as a main course with rice and a salad. If you start with Velvet Limey Soup and finish with Passion Fruit Sorbet you will have a most interesting meal to suit the most discerning of palates. Beware—some people may be allergic to monosodium glutamate. *Serves 4–6 as a starter.*

BATTER
2 egg yolks
50 g (2 oz) plain flour

SAUCE
45 ml (3 tbsp) Japanese soy sauce
5 ml (1 tsp) fresh root ginger, finely grated
15 ml (1 tbsp) caster sugar
30 ml (2 tbsp) sake or sherry
$\frac{1}{4}$ fish or chicken stock cube
pinch monosodium glutamate (optional)
45–60 ml (3–4 tbsp) very finely grated turnip or radish (optional)

USING THE METAL BLADE: make the batter. Place 40–50 ml (1$\frac{1}{2}$–2 fl oz) of iced water, the egg yolks and the flour in the bowl and process until smooth; gradually add another 40–50 ml (1$\frac{1}{2}$–2 fl oz) of iced water until the batter is the consistency of pouring cream. Turn into a bowl.

To make the sauce: combine all the ingredients, except the radish and turnip, in a saucepan with 45–60 ml (3–4 tbsp) of water and bring to the boil. Cool. Serve in little saucers with a little pile of very finely grated turnip or radish in the centre.

If using uncooked prawns, peel them, leaving on the heads. Devein and wash them. Dry on absorbent kitchen paper and season with salt and pepper.

Half peel the aubergine in fine strips and cut into thickish lengthway slices; then cut these into 2–3 pieces, depending on size. Halve the pepper, remove the stalk and seeds and cut into 4 × 6 cm (1$\frac{1}{2}$ × 2$\frac{1}{2}$ inch) pieces. Cut the onion into thick rounds and the courgette into generous slanting slices.

PRAWNS AND VEGETABLES
**8–12 uncooked king prawns or
    cooked prawns
salt
pepper
1 aubergine
1 red or green pepper
1 large sweet onion
1 courgette (optional)
8–12 button mushrooms
vegetable oil, for deep frying**

Heat a deep fryer to 180°C (350°F), or half fill a wok, with oil and heat until just hazing. Dip the prawns into the batter, let the excess drip off then fry until the batter has frizzled and turned golden brown and the prawns are just opaque. Remove and drain on absorbent kitchen paper and keep hot in a hot oven 220°C (425°F) mark 7. Fry all the vegetables in turn and serve as soon as possible after frying. It is best to fry a few pieces and serve them when frying the remainder, but this is not always practical and you may end up with none yourself!

TO SERVE: place the platter of prawn and vegetable tempura in front of the diners who select a piece and dip it into the sauce.

BUTTERSCOTCH APPLE PANCAKES

These sweet pancakes can be flavoured in many different ways. Here they are flavoured with a little coffee and Tia Maria and filled with a butterscotch apple filling which also has a hint of coffee. You could use rum, brandy or Crème de Cacao instead of Tia Maria. They are nice heated in the oven until crisp and served with Sweet Wine Mousseline (page 78). *Serves 4–6.*

BUTTERSCOTCH APPLE FILLING
**50 g (2 oz) butter
100 g (4 oz) light soft brown sugar
50 ml (2 fl oz) single cream or
    milk
700 g (1½ lb) cooking apples
5 ml (1 tsp) instant coffee
¼ tsp vanilla essence**

SWEET PANCAKES
**2 eggs
300 ml (½ pint) milk and water
    mixed
125 g (5 oz) plain flour
15 ml (1 tbsp) light soft brown
    sugar
5 ml (1 tsp) instant coffee
    (optional)
30–45 ml (2–3 tbsp) vegetable oil
15 ml (1 tbsp) Tia Maria**

To make the Butterscotch Apple Filling: place the butter, sugar and cream in a large heavy-based saucepan. Choose one that will be large enough to hold the apples once sliced. Heat gently until the butter melts then stir over a gentle heat until the sugar has melted. Once the sugar has completely dissolved, turn up the heat and boil hard for 1 minute. Meanwhile, peel, core and quarter the apples.

USING THE THICK SLICING DISC: slice the apples using firm pressure on the plunger. Tip all the apples onto the butterscotch mixture, add the instant coffee and vanilla essence and toss all together. Cover and cook for a few minutes until the apples have shed some juice then uncover and continue to cook, stirring frequently, until the apples are well cooked and the mixture is thick.

USING THE METAL BLADE: turn the mixture into the bowl and process until it is smooth but still retains some texture.

USING THE METAL BLADE: make the pancake batter. Place the eggs and half the liquid in the bowl then add the flour, sugar and coffee. Process until smooth then, with the engine running, gradually add the remaining liquid, the oil and the Tia Maria. The batter should be the consistency of thin cream. If necessary, thin it with a little more water.

Lightly grease and heat a 20 cm (8 inch) pan. Pour in about half a coffee cupful of the mixture and swirl around the pan. Cook until lightly brown, turn and cook the other side. Turn out and pile on a plate ready to use. Cool the base of the pan a little before making the next pancake. You should not need to regrease the pan as there is enough fat in the mixture.

Pile some of the butterscotch apple mixture across each pancake, just off centre and roll up. Arrange in a greased shallow ovenproof dish and heat through in a hot oven 220°C (425°F) mark 7 for about 6–8 minutes (allow 10–15 minutes if prepared ahead and cold or use a microwave and then crisp carefully under the grill). Serve with cream or Sweet Wine Mousseline (page 78).

Tutti Frutti Clafoutis

Down in our region of Périgord, a clafoutis is fruit in a good solid flour and egg batter, usually with a splash of *eau de vie*. Although cherries are the classic, apricots and apples follow as close favourites. I have discovered that dried fruit salad makes a wonderful winter clafoutis. *Serves 4–6.*

200 g (7 oz) dried fruits
    eg: prunes, apricots, peaches,
    pears, apples and raisins
cold tea (optional)
sugar (optional)
stick of cinnamon (optional)
strip lemon peel (optional)
3 eggs
50 g (2 oz) plain flour
50 g (2 oz) soft light brown sugar
good pinch salt
450 ml ($\frac{3}{4}$ pint) milk
30–45 ml (2–3 tbsp) *eau de vie*
    or rum

Cover the dried fruit with cold tea or water and leave to soak overnight. Turn into a saucepan, add a little sugar, if desired, the stick of cinnamon and lemon peel, if using, and cook gently until tender. Once tender, drain and place in a greased shallow ovenproof dish.

USING THE METAL BLADE: break the eggs into the bowl, add the flour, sugar, salt and a little of the milk. Process until smooth then add some of the remaining milk with the machine still running. Switch off and stir in the *eau de vie* or rum and remaining milk. Quickly pour the mixture over the fruit and cook in a fairly hot oven 190°C (375°F) mark 5 for about 45 minutes until golden brown and set right through. Leave until lukewarm before serving.

Luxury Praline Filled Pancakes

Fine pancakes filled with a praline butter cream which, when heated in the oven, turn into a glorious sort of nutty crêpe suzette. *Serves 4–6. Makes 12 pancakes.*

PANCAKES
50 g (2 oz) butter
2 eggs
225 ml (8 fl oz) milk
75 g (3 oz) plain flour
2 sugar lumps rubbed on an
    orange until coated in zest
$\frac{1}{4}$ tsp almond essence
$\frac{1}{4}$ tsp salt

PRALINE FILLING
40 g (1$\frac{1}{2}$ oz) flaked almonds
40 g (1$\frac{1}{2}$ oz) whole unskinned
    hazelnuts
100 g (4 oz) caster sugar
100 g (4 oz) unsalted or lightly
    salted soft butter

TO SERVE
icing sugar

Melt the butter until just oiled.

USING THE METAL BLADE: make the pancakes. Place the eggs, about a quarter of the milk, the flour, the sugar lumps with orange zest, almond essence and salt in the bowl. Process until smooth then gradually add in the remaining milk, 50 ml (2 fl oz) of water and the just oiled butter. Turn into a jug. Grease and heat a 15 cm (6 inch) crêpe pan and make 12 thin pancakes. Pile on a plate until ready to use.

To make the praline filling: place the nuts in a frying pan with the sugar; heat until the sugar melts, tipping the pan and stirring very gently with a fork so the nuts and sugar brown evenly. Once the praline is a good caramel brown, turn it out quickly onto a piece of oiled foil; spread thinly and leave until cold and crisp.

USING THE METAL BLADE: break up the praline and process to fine crumbs; set aside. Place the butter in the bowl and process until light and creamy; add in the praline and process to mix.

To assemble the pancakes: lay out the pancakes; put an even-sized blob of filling on each, spread it over half the pancake and fold each pancake into four. Grease a shallow ovenproof dish and lay the pancakes in rows, half overlapping. Cover with cling film until ready to serve.

To serve: remove the cling film, sprinkle heavily with icing sugar and put the pancakes into a hot oven 220°C (425°F) mark 7 for about 5 minutes until crisp, golden and heated through. Serve at once.

DROP SCONES WITH ROSE CREAM AND STRAWBERRIES

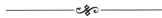

Light and golden drop scones, so good for breakfast or tea, are made with a hint of cinnamon and used as a base for this delicious rose and red wine flavoured cream, topped with fresh strawberries. Cinnamon and rose-water have an affinity, evocative of exotic eastern dishes. (Be cautious when you add rose-water, it is powerful.) They are not unlike *blini*, though much simpler to make. I like to serve them in the same do-it-yourself way, allowing everyone to pile the cream onto their warm drop scone and top it with fruit. You could also serve a choice of sliced fruits or jams. *Serves 4–6. Makes 16 drop scones.*

1 egg
300–350 ml (10–12 fl oz) cultured
    buttermilk or half yogurt and
    half milk
225 g (8 oz) self raising flour
2.5 ml ($\frac{1}{2}$ tsp) bicarbonate of soda
2.5 ml ($\frac{1}{2}$ tsp) cream of tartar
30 ml (2 tbsp) caster sugar
$\frac{1}{4}$ tsp ground cinnamon
    (optional)
15 ml (1 tbsp) sunflower or other
    light vegetable oil
5 ml (1 tsp) rose-water

ROSE CREAM TOPPING
300 ml ($\frac{1}{2}$ pint) double cream
15–30 ml (1–2 tbsp) vanilla sugar
5–10 ml (1–2 tsp) rose-water
60–90 ml (4–6 tbsp) red wine

TO FINISH
500 g (1 lb 2 oz) fresh strawberries
cinnamon sugar (optional)
pepper (optional)

USING THE METAL BLADE: make the drop scones. Place the egg and half the liquid in the bowl. Sift in the flour, bicarbonate of soda and cream of tartar; add the sugar, cinnamon, if using it, oil and rose-water. Process until smooth, stirring down if necessary, then gradually add the remaining liquid until the mixture resembles thick cream. Leave to rest for 10 minutes.

Lightly grease a girdle or heavy frying pan and heat it. Drop tablespoons of the mixture on and cook over a moderate heat for about 2 minutes until the top has just set and the underside is golden. Turn with a palate knife and cook the other side for about 1 minute until it is golden. Wrap in a clean tea towel so they stay moist and tender. If keeping warm or reheating, place the scones in their cloth in a closed container in a very low oven.

USING THE WHISK ATTACHMENT OR A HAND WHISK: make the rose cream topping. Place the cream, sugar, rose-water and red wine in the bowl and whisk until light, airy and holding its shape. Very thick cream may need a little more wine. Do not over beat. Turn into a bowl.

To serve: everyone helps themselves to a drop scone, piles on the cream and tops it with strawberries and, if they like, a sprinkling of cinnamon sugar or a turn of black pepper.

MEAT, CHICKEN AND FISH

The processor is ideal for chopping meat; it does it fast and keeps the meat succulent. You can now make your own homemade minced meat, using the meat of your choice and not the butcher's leftovers. Use it to make Beefburgers (page 40), Koftas (page 43) or Indian-style Kheemas (page 42) as well as your own favourite mince recipes. Raw fish can also be processed successfully in your machine—try turning it into delicate Chinese Crispy Prawn or Scampi Balls (opposite). Not all the recipes mince or chop the meat, for example, Rôti de Porc à la Bourgeoise (page 45) is cooked laid on a variety of processor sliced vegetables.

BAKED FISH WITH WATERCRESS AND ORANGE SAUCE

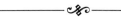

This sauce, with its hint of orange, is delicious over baked fish fillets or served with grilled salmon, turbot or halibut steaks. You can prepare it ahead up to the point of adding the processed watercress leaves to the sauce. The colour of the sauce will dull if left. *Serves 4–6.*

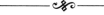

WATERCRESS AND ORANGE SAUCE
1 large orange
30 ml (2 tbsp) vegetable oil
30 ml (2 tbsp) shallot, finely chopped
2–3 bunches watercress
150 ml ($\frac{1}{4}$ pint) dry white wine
150 ml ($\frac{1}{4}$ pint) fish fumet or water and $\frac{1}{2}$ fish stock cube
150 ml ($\frac{1}{4}$ pint) crème fraîche, double or whipping cream
15–25 g ($\frac{1}{2}$–1 oz) butter (optional)
salt
pepper

4–6 fillets or steaks of fresh haddock, cod, salmon, turbot or halibut
30–45 ml (2–3 tbsp) dry white wine or cider
salt
pepper
a little butter

Make the sauce: using a potato peeler or a very sharp knife, pare 3 good strips of orange rind and 1 thumbnail-sized one. Cut the 3 larger strips into needle-sized threads and blanch by bringing to the boil in plenty of cold water; boil for 2–3 minutes then drain and refresh under cold running water. Set aside. Squeeze the orange and reserve the juice.

Heat the oil in a heavy sauté or frying pan and gently soften the shallot in it. Remove the tender sprigs and leaves of watercress and set aside. Roughly cut up the watercress stalks and add them to the pan with the remaining piece of orange rind. Toss in the oil for about $\frac{1}{2}$ minute before adding the wine, orange juice and fish stock. Simmer for 15 minutes or so until very well reduced; then add the cream, bring to the boil, carefully, stirring. Reduce until thick. Strain the sauce, pressing the debris well to extract all the flavour.

Meanwhile, toss the watercress leaves into a pan of boiling, salted water and blanch for 2–5 minutes until just tender. Drain, refresh under cold, running water and press out any excess water.

USING THE METAL BLADE: process the blanched watercress until finely chopped, stopping to stir down if necessary and adding a few drops of sauce. Add in the remaining sauce and process in the butter, if using, and season with salt and pepper. Turn into a saucepan, add the orange rind threads and reheat carefully. Serve in a sauceboat or poured over or spooned onto a plate with the fish steaks arranged in the sauce.

To cook the fish: skin and arrange the fish in a shallow greased ovenproof dish and add the wine or cider, seasoning and a dab of butter. Cover and bake in a moderate oven 180°C (350°F) gas 4 until just done. Add any juices that form to the reducing sauce.

CHINESE CRISPY PRAWN OR SCAMPI BALLS

Golden brown, succulent and tasty, this is a fabulous and authentic Chinese dish that can be served as part of a Chinese meal or with cocktails or as a first course. If you cannot get raw prawns, you can use unbreaded frozen scampi for this dish but allow an extra quarter of the weight for the ice that thaws off them. If you are going to use frozen scampi or prawns, it's best to allow them to thaw for 24 hours in the fridge. This ensures the best texture and flavour. *Makes about 35.*

250 g (9 oz) raw peeled prawns or scampi
50 g (2 oz) back pork fat, diced
2.5 cm (1 inch) cube fresh root ginger, peeled
$\frac{1}{4}$ tsp salt
2 egg whites
30 ml (2 tbsp) cornflour
vegetable oil, for deep frying

Devein and wash the prawns.

USING THE METAL BLADE: process the pork fat until smooth. Add the prawns or scampi and process until smooth, scraping down once. Flatten the cube of ginger with a blow from a heavy cleaver, take the pulp in your hand and hold it over the processor bowl; pour 30 ml (2 tbsp) of cold water over the ginger, squeezing the pulp in your hand (this gives a delicate flavour of ginger) before discarding the ginger pulp. Process in the ginger water, adding the salt. Add alternate spoonfuls of egg white and cornflour as you process. Stop and stir down once and you should have a homogeneous paste which will keep its shape. Heat 5 cm (2 inch) of oil in a wok or deep fryer to 185°C (360°F), just hazing.

Using two wet teaspoons, form balls of the mixture and fry a few at a time in the hot fat for about 2–3 minutes each until a golden brown. Keep hot while frying the remainder and serve at once. For a drinks party, spear on cocktail sticks and hand crushed roasted black or wild pepper mixed with salt round with it.

HAM AND SPINACH LOAF

Leftover ham or the end of a piece of boiled gammon or bacon combined with spinach can be turned into this tasty loaf. *Serves 4–6.*

25 g (1 oz) bread
350 g ($\frac{3}{4}$ lb) cooked ham, gammon or bacon, diced
about 50 g (2 oz) ham fat, diced
100–175 g (4–6 oz) raw spinach leaves, washed and well dried
1 shallot, cut up
small handful parsley heads or other herbs (optional)
1 egg
pepper

USING THE METAL BLADE: process the bread to crumbs and set aside. Process the ham and fat until roughly minced; set aside. Tear the spinach leaves up into the bowl and process with the shallot and parsley until chopped. Return the ham and crumbs to the bowl and add the egg; season with pepper and process until fairly finely chopped and well amalgamated. Turn into a greased 450 g (1 lb) oblong terrine or loaf tin and bake in a fairly hot oven 200°C (400°F) mark 6 for 30–40 minutes until brown and set. It is ready when a skewer inserted comes out clean. Leave to cool. Slice and serve with gherkins, fresh crusty bread and a salad.

BEEFBURGERS

I can no longer stomach cheap commercial beefburgers because I dread to think what goes into them; but I do love juicy tasty home-made ones tucked into a nice soft roll with well fried onions and pickles. Because the food processor chops the meat rather than mincing and squeezing it you get a more succulent result. You can freeze uncooked beefburgers successfully. The onion rings can be sliced using the thick slicing disc on the processor. *Makes 4.*

FRIED ONIONS
2–3 large onions, skinned
30–45 ml (2–3 tbsp) vegetable oil
5 ml (1 tsp) sugar

BEEFBURGERS
450 g (1 lb) beef trimmed of
    sinew and gristle (buttock,
    chuck, or flank); $\frac{4}{5}$ lean meat to
    $\frac{1}{5}$ fat
$\frac{1}{4}$ onion, skinned
1 slice bread, broken up
small handful fresh herbs eg:
    parsley, marjoram or thyme or
    a pinch of dried mixed herbs
    (optional)
2.5 ml ($\frac{1}{2}$ tsp) salt
pepper
1 egg
vegetable oil, for frying

TO SERVE
4 large soft buns, warmed
4 tomatoes, sliced
pickled dill cucumber
pickles and relishes

Start by frying the onions for serving with the beefburgers.

USING THE THICK SLICING DISC: halve and slice the onions with firm pressure on the plunger. Heat the fat in a large frying pan or sauté pan, put in the onion slices and fry over a moderate heat. Sprinkle them with sugar to help them brown; they will take 20 minutes or more to become a nice golden brown; remove and keep warm.

Remove and discard the sinew and gristle from the beef. Cut it into cubes.

USING THE METAL BLADE: with the engine running, drop half the beef quickly down the feed tube. Process until finely chopped but not too finely. Remove and chop the next batch. (Larger machines will do all this quantity at once.) Remove the meat.

Place the onion and broken bread in the bowl with the herbs and process until finely chopped.

USING THE PLASTIC BLADE: return the meat to the bowl with the onion, bread and herbs, add salt and pepper and the egg and process until well mixed. Alternatively, mix together by hand.

Moisten your hands with cold water and form into four flattish beefburgers. Cook either on a hot barbecue or lightly grease a frying pan and heat until smokingly hot. You can also use a ribbed grill pan, which will give you a nice lattice pattern on the beefburgers if you shift them a quarter turn half way through the cooking time for each side. Cook the beefburgers for 3–4 minutes on each side; don't overcook or they will get dry and hard.

To serve: split the warmed buns, pop in a beefburger, top with the browned onion rings and serve with sliced tomatoes, pickled dill cucumber and relishes.

INDONESIAN SATÉ WITH YELLOW RICE

This dish is lovely for a summer barbecue party. Cubes of meat are tenderised in a delicate coconut marinade, grilled crispy brown and then served on a bed of turmeric and coconut-flavoured rice with a creamy peanut sauce. If you cannot get creamed coconut, you can make your own (page 12). *Serves 4–6.*

50 g (2 oz) packet creamed
    coconut
grated rind and juice 1 lime or
    lemon
salt
pinch of chilli or cayenne
800 g–1 kg (1¾–2 lb) lean pork,
    veal or chicken breast, cubed

SATÉ SAUCE
15 ml (1 tbsp) peanut oil or any
    light vegetable oil
3 cloves garlic, peeled
90 ml (6 tbsp) peanut butter or
    100 g (4 oz) salted peanuts
400 ml (14 fl oz) chicken stock or
    water
½ chicken stock cube
good pinch sugar (optional)
salt, if necessary
chilli or cayenne, to taste
grated rind and juice of ½–1 lime
    or lemon

YELLOW RICE
100 g (4 oz) packet creamed
    coconut
350 g (12 oz) long grain rice,
    washed
5 ml (1 tsp) turmeric
1 bay leaf
1 chicken stock cube

GARNISH (OPTIONAL)
lime shreds
sprigs watercress or celery leaf
strips of red pepper
crispy brown fried onion rings
omelette strips
roughly chopped parsley
roasted peanuts

USING THE METAL BLADE: process the creamed coconut with 50 ml (2 fl oz) of hot water, lime rind and juice, salt and chilli until smooth; then combine with the meat, mix well and leave to marinate for at least 1 hour. Thread on to skewers and barbecue or grill on a high heat, brushing with the marinade. Cook until brown but still succulent.

To make saté sauce: heat the oil in a pan and gently fry the garlic in it until golden.

USING THE METAL BLADE: add the garlic and the peanut butter (or peanuts) and process until as smooth as possible. Gradually add the stock or water, stock cube, sugar, salt and chilli. Sieve into a saucepan and simmer, stirring occasionally, for 5–10 minutes. The sauce should be a coating consistency. Finish by adding the grated lime rind and juice.

USING THE METAL BLADE: make the yellow rice. Process the creamed coconut, gradually adding 300 ml (½ pint) of hot water to make a smooth mixture.

Turn into a large saucepan and add 450 ml (¾ pint) of water and the rice; add the turmeric, bay leaf and crumbled stock cube. Bring to the boil, add some salt, if necessary, and boil briskly, uncovered, for 8–10 minutes until steam holes appear in the rice. Cover and leave over a very low heat for 15–20 minutes until all the liquid has been absorbed and the rice is dry. Toss with a fork and turn onto a serving dish. Garnish, if you wish, with sprigs of watercress and celery leaf, red pepper strips, crispy brown fried onion rings, omelette strips, roughly chopped parsley and roasted peanuts. Top with the skewers of grilled meat.

See illustration facing page 33

Kheema with Lettuce

Kheema is a dry, curried Indian mince to which vegetables like peas, diced potato, okra, or spinach can be added. It also makes a nice filling for samosas. I like to serve the kheema with crisp lettuce leaves just as the Chinese serve a minced pigeon dish. You place a spoonful of kheema on a crisp lettuce leaf, top it with a spoonful of thick yogurt, fold it up and eat it with your fingers; the contrast of hot and spicy and cool and crisp is excellent. You can add little dabs of lime pickle to your parcel or serve the kheema and lettuce in Pitta Bread (page 86) or with rice. *Serves 4.*

2 onions, skinned
30 ml (2 tbsp) vegetable oil
450 g (1 lb) boneless and lean
    lamb or beef, cubed
10 ml (2 tsp) coriander seeds
1–2 fresh chillies, deseeded,
    or $\frac{1}{4}$–$\frac{1}{2}$ tsp ground chilli
    or cayenne
2–3 cloves garlic, peeled
15 ml (1 tbsp) fresh root ginger,
    grated
5 ml (1 tsp) cumin seeds
2.5 ml ($\frac{1}{2}$ tsp) turmeric
300 ml ($\frac{1}{2}$ pint) stock or water
salt
15–30 ml (1–2 tbsp) fresh
    coriander or parsley, chopped
15–30 ml (1–2 tbsp) lemon juice

TO SERVE
1 head lettuce, washed
250 ml (8 fl oz) thick yogurt

USING THE METAL BLADE: quarter the onions into the bowl and chop roughly, using the on/off or pulse technique. Heat the oil in a wide frying pan and fry the onion in it to a light brown. With the engine running, add half the meat down the feed tube and process until minced. Do not over-process. Remove and chop the remaining meat in the machine. (Large machines may do all the meat at once). Over a high heat, add the meat to the pan and stir and toss for several minutes until lightly browned. Pound the coriander seeds in a pestle and mortar. Finely chop the chilli and garlic by hand (beware, chilli can burn), and add with the ginger, crushed coriander seeds, cumin seeds and turmeric to the pan; fry for 1–2 minutes. Add the stock and salt. Cover and simmer for 15–30 minutes until the mince is tender, adding more liquid if it dries out before it is tender. Once tender, add the chopped coriander and lemon juice and cook over a high heat until the liquid has all reduced away. Mound onto a serving dish and serve piping hot with the lettuce and yogurt handed round in separate bowls.

Smoked Sausage and Cabbage Leaf Cake

Smoked garlic sausage gives a lovely flavour to these stuffed cabbage leaves which end up coated with a trace of tomato sauce and are turned out and cut like a cake. *Serves 4–6.*

10–12 good savoy or green
    cabbage leaves
salt
1 onion, skinned and cut up
15 ml (1 tbsp) vegetable oil or
    dripping
100 g (4 oz) long grain rice
200 g (7 oz) smoked garlic
    sausage ring, skinned, cut up
1 egg
pepper

Blanch the cabbage leaves in plenty of boiling salted water until they are just limp and flexible. Drain, refresh under running cold water and drain.

USING THE METAL BLADE: process the onion with the on/off or pulse technique until evenly but roughly chopped. Heat the oil in a saucepan and fry the onion in it until soft and golden; then stir in the rice and toss until it glistens all over. Add 200 ml (7 fl oz) of water and boil, covered, for about 10 minutes or until the water is absorbed.

USING THE METAL BLADE: process the smoked garlic sausage until finely chopped. Add the half cooked rice, the egg and plenty of salt and pepper and process just long enough to combine.

SAUCE

**2 slices cut from a thin skinned
 lemon**

30 ml (2 tbsp) tomato purée

salt

pepper

Grease a 20–23 cm (8–9 inch) round ovenproof gratin dish and line with about two-thirds of the cabbage leaves, letting them hang over the rim. Pack in the filling and cover with the remaining leaves, folding in the leaves hanging over the rim.

USING THE METAL BLADE: make the sauce. Process the lemon slices with the tomato purée and then trickle in 200 ml (7 fl oz) of water. Season and strain this sauce over the cabbage cake. Cover the cake lightly with a butter paper or tinfoil, but don't seal the edges and cook in a fairly hot oven 190°C (375°F) mark 5 for about 1 hour. You will find that the sauce will have soaked in, leaving a red tinge on the cabbage. Turn out onto a warm serving dish and serve, sliced, like a cake.

TINY LAMB KOFTAS WITH TOMATO SAUCE

Koftas, which are spicy meatballs, are a Middle Eastern dish. They can be served as an appetiser on sticks, as a main course dipped into tomato sauce, or stuffed into Pitta Bread (page 86). *Serves 4.*

**500 g (1 lb 2 oz) boned shoulder
 or leg of lamb**

1–2 cloves garlic, roughly cut up

**handful fresh parsley or
 coriander leaves**

**15 ml (1 tbsp) fresh root ginger,
 grated**

good pinch ground cinnamon

**2.5 ml ($\frac{1}{2}$ tsp) pounded cumin
 seeds**

2.5–5 ml ($\frac{1}{2}$–1 tsp) curry powder

5 ml (1 tsp) salt

**1 fresh chilli, deseeded,
 chopped or $\frac{1}{4}$ tsp cayenne**

**30–45 ml (2–3 tbsp) yogurt or
 cold water**

vegetable oil, for frying

paprika

$\frac{1}{2}$ lemon

TOMATO SAUCE

30 ml (2 tbsp) olive oil

**1 onion, skinned and finely
 chopped**

1 clove garlic, finely chopped

**400 g (14 oz) can tomatoes or
 450 g (1 lb) fresh tomatoes**

15 ml (1 tbsp) tomato purée

$\frac{1}{4}$ tsp dried oregano

5 ml (1 tsp) sugar

salt

pepper

Remove all gristle and sinew from the meat but leave a little fat. Cube the meat and mix with the garlic and parsley or coriander leaves.

USING THE METAL BLADE: quickly drop the meat, garlic and herbs down the feed tube onto the moving blades. Process until finely minced then add the ginger, cinnamon, cumin, curry powder, salt and chilli or cayenne and the yogurt or water. Process until very smooth. Using wet fingers, form into marble-sized balls.

Pour 0.5 cm ($\frac{1}{4}$ inch) of oil into a frying pan or alternatively pour 75–90 ml (5–6 tbsp) of oil into a wok and heat. When hot, fry the koftas, shaking and rolling them around the pan until golden brown but still moist and succulent inside. Keep hot. Just before serving, sprinkle them generously with paprika and squeeze over a little lemon juice.

To make the tomato sauce: heat the oil in a saucepan, add the onion and garlic and fry until golden.

USING THE METAL BLADE: place the drained tomatoes in the food processor bowl and process until smooth, then add in their juice. Strain. Add the tomato purée to the onions and fry for a moment before adding the tomato pulp, the oregano, sugar, salt and pepper. Simmer until it reduces to a tasty sauce. Serve the koftas hot with the tomato sauce.

LAMB WITH AUBERGINE, GARLIC AND TAHINA SAUCE

A head of garlic may sound a lot but, blanched and slowly cooked with the lamb and aubergine, it gives a delicate flavour. The tahina (sesame paste) adds an interesting flavour and smooth texture to the finished sauce. I usually make this with generously cut cubes of meat but sometimes use a whole leg and adjust the cooking time. *Serves 4–6.*

1 large aubergine, about
    300–400 g (11–14 oz), cut to fit
    the feed tube
salt
1 head firm, fresh garlic, peeled
30–45 ml (2–3 tbsp) olive oil
1 kg (2 lb) boneless shoulder or
    leg of lamb, cut into 4 cm
    (1½ inch) cubes
2 onions, skinned and halved
2 slices cut from thin-skinned
    lemon
pepper
30–45 ml (2–3 tbsp) tahina
juice of ½–1 lemon

USING THE CHIPPER OR THICK SLICING DISC: chip or slice the aubergine with medium pressure on the plunger. Layer the aubergine slices in a colander, sprinkling each layer with salt; press with a saucer and weights and leave to disgorge for 30 minutes. Rinse off the salt and pat dry.

Pull the head of garlic apart and throw the cloves into a saucepan filled with plenty of cold water. Bring to the boil, boil for 1 minute and discard the water; peel the garlic and set aside.

Heat the oil in a heavy, flameproof casserole or frying pan and brown the meat cubes in it. Remove with a slotted spoon and set aside.

USING THE THICK SLICING DISC: slice the onions, add to the oil in the pan, adding a little more if necessary, and cook gently until soft and golden. Add the aubergine to the pan and toss around for 1 or 2 minutes until the oil is absorbed.

Return the lamb to the pan, add the garlic cloves and the slices of lemon; season lightly with salt and pepper, cover closely and cook in a moderate oven 180°C (350°F) mark 4 for about 1–1½ hours until the meat is tender. Pick out the pieces of meat and keep hot. Drain off the liquid and degrease.

USING THE METAL BLADE: process the solids from the sauce and add the tahina. Once smooth, add the reserved liquid down the feed tube with the machine running. Then return the sauce through a sieve to the rinsed out casserole; if too thick, add a little liquid. If the sauce is too thin, boil it hard to reduce, stirring so that it does not catch. Once you have achieved a good coating consistency, correct the seasoning, add lemon juice to taste and return the lamb cubes. Reheat and serve. This dish can be kept warm and will also reheat well.

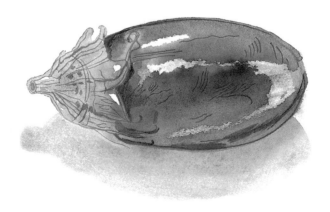

RÔTI DE PORC À LA BOURGEOISE

This has the lovely rich flavours of good French country cooking. The seasoned meat can be stuffed with an onion and rosemary stuffing if you wish; it is then roasted on a bed of thick, food processor-sliced vegetables which acquire a deep flavour from the pork drippings. Choose a pork joint with some but not too much fat and if you roast a larger joint, give it half an hour or so in the oven and pour off the fat before putting it on the bed of vegetables. Leg or shoulder of lamb can also be cooked this way. *Serves 6–8.*

6–8 peppercorns
1–2 cloves garlic, skinned
½ bay leaf, broken up
3–4 juniper berries
7 ml (1½ tsp) salt
1.6–1.8 kg (3½–4 lb) spare rib joint
    of pork, boned and scored

STUFFING (OPTIONAL)
200 g (7 oz) onions, skinned and
    cut up
40 g (1½ oz) dripping, fat or
    vegetable oil
2–3 slices stale brown or white
    bread
2.5 ml (½ tsp) very finely chopped
    rosemary
1 egg
salt
pepper

SLICED VEGETABLES
1–2 medium aubergines
salt
750 g–1 kg (1½–2 lb) potatoes,
    peeled
350 g (¾ lb) onions
1–2 medium red or green peppers
vegetable oil

Crush the peppercorns in a mortar then add the garlic, bay leaf and juniper berries; crush these then gradually work in the salt. Rub this seasoning mixture well into the pork. Set it aside in a cool place for 4–24 hours.

USING THE FINE SLICING DISC: make the stuffing, if liked. Slice the onions with firm pressure. Heat the fat in a frying pan over a moderate heat and cook the onions in it until soft golden brown.

USING THE METAL BLADE: process the bread to crumbs, add in the onion, rosemary, egg, salt and pepper and process, briefly, until amalgamated. Stuff this mixture into the cavity of the seasoned joint (in some joints you will have to cut a pocket) and sew or skewer together. Tie in 2–3 places to make a good shape.

USING THE THICKEST SLICING DISC: prepare the vegetable accompaniment. Cut the aubergines in half lengthways and slice using firm pressure; layer in a colander, sprinkling each layer with salt; press with a plate and weight and leave to disgorge their bitter juices for 30 minutes. Rinse off the salt and pat dry.

USING THE THICKEST SLICING DISC: slice half the potatoes and spread over the base of a greased 30–35 cm (12 × 14 inch) roasting pan or earthenware gratin dish. Slice the onions and spread over the potatoes. Cut the peppers in half lengthways, remove the seeds and core and pack firmly upright in the feed tube. Slice with firm pressure and scatter over the onion. Add in the aubergine slices. Don't worry if the vegetables get all mixed up. Season lightly and top with the remaining sliced potatoes which should cover the other vegetables so they don't get dry. Brush the potatoes with oil and set the roast in the middle. Roast in a moderate oven 180°C (350°F) mark 4, allowing 25–30 minutes for each 450 g (1 lb) of meat. Turn the heat up to 230°C (450°F) mark 8 for the last 20–30 minutes to allow the crackling to bubble and crispen. If the vegetables seem done, and they should be nice and crisp and brown at the edges, you may have to transfer the meat to another roasting pan to finish cooking.

VEAL FRIKADELLA WITH MUSHROOM SAUCE

These Scandinavian patties of minced veal are very moist and succulent and have a delicate flavour. The mixture is almost like a quenelle and is ideal for making in the food processor. *Serves 4–6.*

450 g (1 lb) lean pie or stewing
    veal, cubed
2 slices white bread
60–90 ml (4–6 tbsp) soured
    cream, crème fraîche, cream or
    milk
4 egg whites
a little finely grated lemon rind
a good pinch ground mace
salt
pepper
flour, for coating
50 g (2 oz) butter
15 ml (1 tbsp) vegetable oil

SAUCE
100 g (4 oz) firm button
    mushrooms
15 ml (1 tbsp) very finely
    chopped shallot
$\frac{1}{4}$ tsp potato flour
150 ml ($\frac{1}{4}$ pint) whipping cream
salt and pepper
squeeze lemon juice

USING THE METAL BLADE: turn on the machine and feed half the meat onto the moving blades. Process only until medium finely chopped, then remove. Chop the remaining meat in same way and remove. (In large machines, the meat can be done in one go.)

Remove the crusts from the bread and soak in the cream. Process the egg whites until foamy, then add the bread and cream and process again. Return all the meat to the bowl and add the lemon rind, mace, salt and pepper. Process until all is well mixed but do not over-process or chop the meat too finely. Leave the mixture to rest for 30 minutes. Take good spoonfuls of the mixture, form into 1–2 cm ($\frac{1}{2}$–$\frac{3}{4}$ inch) thick patties and roll in flour. In a frying pan heat the butter and oil and when hot add the meat and fry briskly until golden brown on both sides. Remove with a slotted spoon and keep warm. Keep the fat in the pan and use it for making the sauce.

USING THE THIN SLICING BLADE: make the sauce. Stack the button mushrooms sideways in the feed tube and slice, using firm pressure on the plunger. Reheat the fat in the pan and add the shallot to it; soften gently for 1 minute then add the mushrooms and fry for about 1 minute. Mix the potato flour into the cream and add to the pan; season with a little salt and pepper. Boil up, stirring hard until you have a smooth coating sauce; then add a squeeze of lemon juice and pour over the frikadella. Serve at once.

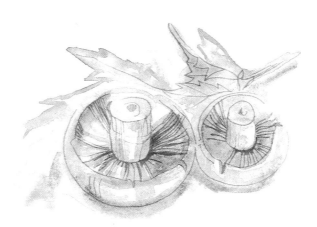

STIR-FRIED TURKEY BREAST WITH VEGETABLES AND BLACK BEAN SAUCE

Fermented black beans are a passion of mine. Their special piquant flavour enhances Chinese dishes of fish, prawn, beef or, in this case, turkey fillet and sliced mixed vegetables. They are available from Oriental stores. This takes only moments to cook, and with the food processor to do the slicing, not too long to prepare. *Serves 4–6.*

350–450 g (12–16 oz) turkey or chicken breast

SEASONING
30 ml (2 tbsp) soy sauce
15 ml (1 tbsp) white wine or sherry
1.25–2.5 ml ($\frac{1}{4}$–$\frac{1}{2}$ tsp) salt
5 ml (1 tsp) ginger juice, made by squeezing ginger in a garlic press
15 ml (1 tbsp) cornflour

BLACK BEANS
45 ml (3 tbsp) fermented black beans
15 ml (1 tbsp) oil
5 ml (1 tsp) sugar
30 ml (2 tbsp) white wine or sherry

VEGETABLES (some or all of these)
1–2 onions, peeled
100 g (4 oz) turnips, peeled
200 g (7 oz) carrots, scraped and peeled
3–4 large firm Chinese leaves
3–4 sticks celery
1 green pepper, halved and seeded

1 red chilli, seeded and finely chopped
1 clove garlic, peeled and finely chopped
2–3 slices fresh ginger root, peeled and cut into shreds

SAUCE
150 ml ($\frac{1}{4}$ pint) chicken stock
15 ml (1 tbsp) cornflour
15 ml (1 tbsp) soya sauce
2.5 ml ($\frac{1}{2}$ tsp) sugar
1.25–2.5 ml ($\frac{1}{4}$–$\frac{1}{2}$ tsp) salt
few drops sesame oil (optional)

Remove the skin and slice the turkey or chicken breast into thin strips. Mix with all the seasoning ingredients and leave to stand for at least 15 minutes.

Place the black beans, oil, sugar and wine in a small bowl and steam, covered, standing on a trivet over boiling water for 3 minutes; set aside.

USING THE STANDARD SLICING DISC: halve the onions and turnips, or cut to fit the feed tube, pack carefully in the feed tube and slice with moderate pressure. Pack the carrots, some thick ends up, some thick ends down and slice with moderate pressure; set aside.

USING THE 6 mm EXTRA THICK SLICING DISC: pack the Chinese leaves in the feed tube with the celery sticks and slice with firm pressure. If you have no extra thick slicing disc, slice the Chinese leaves and celery by hand. Pack the pepper tightly in the feed tube and slice with moderate pressure. Mix together the sauce ingredients in a small bowl.

Heat the oil in a wok or large frying pan and when very hot and just hazing, add half the turkey strips; stir to separate and fry for about $\frac{1}{2}$ minute until firm and just browning at the edges. Remove with a slotted spoon and drain on kitchen paper. Cook the remaining turkey strips in the same way and drain.

Pour off all but about 30 ml (2 tbsp) of the oil from the wok or frying pan, then reheat the pan. When hazing, add the onion, turnips and carrot slices. Stir-fry over high heat for 1–2 minutes, then add the chilli, garlic, ginger shreds, Chinese leaves, celery and green pepper slices. Stir-fry for another minute or so, then add the black bean preparation and the reserved turkey shreds. Stir and add the sauce ingredients. Toss and cook all together for 1 minute until heated through and the sauce has thickened. Turn into a heated serving dish and serve at once.

PIQUANT CHICKEN CROÛTES

Leftover cooked chicken is excellent processed with a piquant mayonnaise to top croûtes, biscuits or bread. Lime pickle is the secret ingredient that gives the mixture its kick. You can also use leftover turkey, pork, veal or ham equally successfully. *Serves 4 as a snack.*

150 ml ($\frac{1}{4}$ pint) mayonnaise
1 clove garlic, peeled and
    chopped
1 thin slice onion
10–15 ml (2–3 tsp) chopped mild
    lime pickle
15–30 ml (1–2 tbsp) tomato
    ketchup
5 ml (1 tsp) Dijon mustard
salt
pepper
2.5 ml ($\frac{1}{2}$ tsp) wine vinegar,
    to taste
250 g (9 oz) cooked chicken,
    skinned and diced

TO SERVE
croûtes of granary or ryebread,
    little biscuits or oatcakes or
    slices of bread, for open
    sandwiches

USING THE METAL BLADE: put the mayonnaise in the bowl and add the garlic, onion, lime pickle, tomato ketchup, mustard, salt, pepper and vinegar. Process until smooth, adjust the seasoning then add the chicken. Process with the on/off or pulse technique, stirring down if necessary, until fairly finely chopped but not too smooth. At the last moment, pile this mixture onto toasted circles of granary or rye bread or onto small water biscuits or oatcakes.

VELVET CHICKEN WITH BROCCOLI

Without a food processor, this Chinese dish takes hours of preparation. The processor is perfect for chopping the chicken breast meat so smoothly that it takes on a velvety texture. The cooking temperature is critical for perfect results. *Serves 4–6 with other dishes.*

225 g ($\frac{1}{2}$ lb) chicken breast, boned
    and skinned
3 egg whites
5 ml (1 tsp) cornflour
2.5 ml ($\frac{1}{2}$ tsp) salt
vegetable oil, for frying

SAUCE
225 g ($\frac{1}{2}$ lb) broccoli, cut into
    florets, or mange-tout
10 ml (2 tsp) chicken fat or
    vegetable oil
10 ml (2 tsp) cornflour
150 ml ($\frac{1}{4}$ pint) good strong
    chicken stock

USING THE METAL BLADE: process the chicken breast to a smooth paste, dripping in 15 ml (1 tbsp) of iced water. Pick out any threads or ligaments if you see them then add the egg whites, cornflour and salt and process briefly until the mixture is smooth and homogeneous. In a wok or heavy pan, pour in oil to a depth of 2 cm (1 inch) and heat to 74°C (165°F), stir and keep at this temperature. Drop carefully formed, almond shaped half teaspoonfuls of the mixture into the warm oil. Remove the pieces after 10–15 seconds once they go white and *just* become firm (if they brown or the mixture is bubbly when cut, the oil is too warm). Drain well. This can be done ahead and then the chicken drops can be reheated in the sauce.

    To make the sauce: cook the broccoli lightly in boiling salty water with a few drops of oil added. Drain and refresh. Mix the chicken fat, cornflour and stock together and bring to the boil in a wok or wide frying pan; toss in the broccoli and chicken drops and heat gently. Serve at once.

CHICKEN IN A CREAMY CASHEW NUT SAUCE

Delicately spiced dishes are one of my passions; this one uses processed cashew nuts which both flavour and thicken the sauce. It is one of those useful dishes that is best made ahead, allowing time for the flavours to blend. Cashew nuts are expensive but you can buy cheaper small or broken cashew nuts from health shops which will do well for this recipe. *Serves 4–6.*

4–6 chicken portions
about 900 ml (1½ pints) chicken
   stock or water
½ chicken stock cube
2 slices root ginger
1 fresh or dried chilli
1 clove garlic, peeled
1 onion skinned, halved, stuck
   with 2 cloves
1 carrot
salt
pepper

CASHEW NUT SAUCE
2 medium onions, skinned and
   cut up
2 cloves garlic, peeled
2–3 cm (¾–1 inch) slice root
   ginger
30 ml (2 tbsp) ghee or vegetable
   oil
¼ tsp ground cardamom
2.5 ml (½ tsp) garam masala
50 g (2 oz) cashew nuts, almonds
   or peanuts
squeeze lime or lemon juice
salt
pepper

TO GARNISH
a few browned cashew nuts

Just cover the chicken portions in stock or water and poach with the stock cube, ginger, chilli, garlic, onion halves, carrot and seasoning. When cooked, drain off the stock and reduce to about 450 ml (¾ pint). Discard the seasoning ingredients. Cut up the chicken.

USING THE METAL BLADE: make the sauce. Roughly chop the onions, garlic and ginger in the food processor using the on/off or pulse technique for an even chop. Heat the ghee or oil in a saucepan and, when hot, fry this mixture in it for about 10 minutes or so until soft and golden, adding in the cardamom and garam masala for the last 1–2 minutes. Process the cashew nuts until they form a paste; return the onion-spice mixture to the bowl and process until smooth, gradually adding in about 350 ml (12 fl oz) of the reduced chicken stock. Return the sauce to the pan and heat gently, stirring all the time, until it simmers and thickens; correct the seasoning. Return the chicken pieces to the sauce. Leave for a few minutes for the flavours to blend or preferably leave overnight and reheat gently. Just before serving, add a good squeeze of lime or lemon juice. Serve scattered with browned cashew nuts.

Spiced chocolate cake (page 90)

Overleaf: Chicken salad with avocado and ricotta sauce (page 53) and green coleslaw with mustard and brown sugar dressing (page 52)

SALADS AND VEGETABLES

For the health-conscious person who enjoys vegetables a processor really comes into its own. The different blades will give you a tremendous variety of textures and sizes of shreds, slices, chips and bits which you can use to make a wonderful range of salads and vegetable dishes. Many of these can be served as a main course. Just let your imagination go. And for dressings you can let your own ideas take over, incorporating herbs, nuts, eggs, olives and anchovies to give your dressings individuality.

PASTA SHELL SALAD

Cold ham, leftover roast beef, pork or veal, garlic sausage or any combination of these can be made into an appetising salad when mixed with cooked pasta shells and dressed. *Serves 4–6.*

DRESSING
150 ml (¼ pint) mayonnaise
   (page 72)
1 clove garlic, peeled and finely
   chopped
10 ml (2 tsp) mild paprika
15 ml (1 tbsp) wine vinegar
5 ml (1 tsp) Dijon mustard
a handful of celery leaves and/or
   other herbs
30–45 ml (2–3 tbsp) yogurt
salt
pepper

100 g (4 oz) firm button
   mushrooms, washed or wiped
1 small head celery
200 – 350 g (7–12 oz) cooked meat,
   diced
100 g (4 oz) pasta shells, cooked

TO GARNISH
1 bunch watercress (optional)

USING THE THICK SLICING BLADE: carefully pack the mushrooms sideways in the feed tube and slice with moderate pressure. Slice the tender celery stalks, but reserve the leaves. Turn into a bowl and add the meat and pasta shells.

USING THE METAL BLADE: make the dressing. Place all the dressing ingredients in the bowl and process together until the herbs are finely chopped; adjust the seasoning.

Spoon the dressing over the salad. Toss well and arrange attractively, garnished with watercress, if liked, and serve.

Carrot, Sultana and Coriander Salad

This is a simple grated salad. You could vary it by using some parsnip, celeriac or turnip in place of the carrots, if you like. You could also add some roasted almonds or hazelnuts or toasted sunflower seeds or you could add chopped fresh coriander or celery leaves. It is also nice to plump up the sultanas in orange juice before adding to the salad. If you are using young soft carrots grate them as coarsely as possible as they can give out a great deal of moisture if grated too finely. *Serves 4–6.*

500–750 g (1–1½ lb) young carrots, scrubbed or peeled
50 g (2 oz) sultanas

CORIANDER AND ORANGE DRESSING
10 ml (2 tsp) coriander seeds
handful parsley (optional)
1 sugar lump, rubbed on an orange until covered in zest, crushed
½ shallot or very small onion, skinned and roughly cut up
1 clove garlic
2.5 ml (½ tsp) salt
pepper
150 ml (¼ pint) crème fraîche, soured cream or yogurt

USING THE MEDIUM OR COARSE GRATING DISC OR THE JULIENNE DISC: cut the carrots to lie crossways in the feed tube. Stack the tube and grate, using firm pressure on the plunger. Put the carrot shreds in a bowl and add the sultanas.

To make the dressing: roast the coriander seeds in a heavy frying pan, over a moderate heat, shaking constantly. Do this until they darken a little and smell roasted. Crush in a pestle and mortar.

USING THE METAL BLADE: place the parsley, if using it, roasted coriander, sugar cube, shallot, garlic, salt and pepper in the processor bowl and process until finely chopped. With the engine running, pour in the crème fraîche and switch off the moment it thickens. If you over-process the mixture could curdle. Commercial soured cream or yogurt will only thin out if processed so just stir the dressing ingredients into them. Pour the dressing over the carrots and toss well. Serve at once or keep for several hours for the flavours to blend.

Raw Beetroot Salad with Horseradish and Walnut Oil

Beetroot is usually eaten cooked but when it is young, it makes a lovely raw salad. The fine crimson ribbons only need dressing with some really good oil and a little horseradish or dill and capers. Serve as a salad, as part of a mixed hors d'oeuvre or in a dish of contrasting salads. *Serves 4–6.*

400–500 g (14 oz–1 lb 2 oz) young, firm beetroot, peeled
a little finely grated fresh horseradish or 10–15 ml (2 tsp) creamed horseradish
15–20 ml (3–4 tsp) wine vinegar
45–60 ml (3–4 tbsp) walnut, hazelnut or olive oil
salt
pepper

USING THE FINE OR STANDARD GRATING DISC: grate the beetroot using firm pressure on the plunger. Mix it with the horseradish, vinegar and oil. Season and toss well.

TOMATO AND SWEET ONION SALAD WITH CREAM CHEESE DRESSING

If you can get mild sweet onions, especially the red skinned kind, do use them in this tasty tomato salad with a cream cheese dressing. *Serves 4–6.*

500 g (1 lb 2 oz) ripe, firm
    tomatoes
1–2 sweet onions, skinned and
    halved

DRESSING
50 g (2 oz) full fat soft cheese
¼ tsp paprika
small handful chervil or parsley
45 ml (3 tbsp) tarragon vinegar
sprig tarragon (optional)
135 ml (9 tbsp) sunflower oil
salt
pepper

TO GARNISH
chives

In a bowl, cover the tomatoes with boiling water for 30 seconds. Drain and plunge into cold water. Peel and slice thinly, by hand, into a shallow dish.

USING THE FINEST SLICING DISC: slice the onions, using light pressure on the plunger. Scatter the onion over the tomatoes.

USING THE METAL BLADE: place the cream cheese, paprika, herbs, vinegar and seasoning in the bowl; process briefly until smooth then add the oil in a steady stream. Do not overprocess or the mixture might curdle. Pour the dressing over the centre of the dish and scissor chives around the edge.

GREEN COLESLAW WITH MUSTARD AND BROWN SUGAR DRESSING

White cabbage and savoy are best sliced finely with the standard slicing disc for if you use the coleslaw cutter, which virtually grates them, you get a rather heavy salad which is inclined to be wet. It is good, however, for coarse grating carrots, turnips, kohlrabi, celeriac and parsnips, all of which are nice in a coleslaw. *Serves 4–6.*

MUSTARD AND BROWN SUGAR
DRESSING
1 egg
15 ml (1 tbsp) coarse-grained
    mustard
45 ml (3 tbsp) soft dark brown
    sugar
5 ml (1 tsp) plain flour
50 ml (2 fl oz) tarragon vinegar
30 ml (2 tbsp) sunflower oil
¼ tsp salt
pepper
75 ml (3 fl oz) milk or whipping
    cream

USING THE METAL BLADE: make the dressing. Put the egg, mustard, sugar, flour, vinegar, oil and the salt and pepper in the bowl and process for about 30 seconds. Turn into a heavy-based saucepan and bring to a simmer, stirring or whisking all the time; simmer until the mixture boils and thickens then turn into a bowl and stir in the milk or cream. Leave to cool.

USING THE STANDARD SLICING BLADE: cut the cabbage into columns which will fit the food processor tube, cut out the stalk and slice with light pressure on the plunger. Turn into a salad bowl.

USING THE COARSE GRATING BLADE OR COLESLAW CUTTER: cut the turnips, if large, to fit the tube and grate with moderate pressure on the plunger. Add to the cabbage.
See illustration facing page 48

GREEN COLESLAW

$\frac{1}{2}$ small white or savoy cabbage

1–2 young turnips

8–10 cm (3–4 inch) cucumber

2–3 sticks celery

1 tart green apple, cored

$\frac{1}{4}$–$\frac{1}{2}$ green pepper, deseeded

$\frac{1}{2}$ bunch watercress, washed and
dried (optional)

USING THE THICK SLICING BLADE: cut the cucumber into four lengthways and pack upright in the tube with the celery sticks. Slice using firm pressure. Cut the apple into sixths or eighths lengthways, depending on size; stack upright in the feed tube with the halved or quartered pepper and slice with firm pressure. Turn into the salad bowl, add sprigs of watercress, if using, and toss with the dressing.

CHICKEN SALAD WITH AVOCADO AND RICOTTA SAUCE

This is my own special way of poaching chicken, which makes the chicken very moist. It is served while tepid with a delicate avocado and ricotta cheese sauce. It makes a most attractive summer dish. Avocado discolours quickly so do not make the sauce too far in advance. Fine rings of fresh chilli make an attractive garnish, but may be too hot for some tastes. Red and green pepper strips would make a good substitute. *Serves 4–8.*

2 spring onions

1–2 carrots, roughly chopped

1 stick celery, roughly chopped

2.5 litres (4$\frac{1}{4}$ pints) light chicken
stock or water and 1 stock cube

2–3 slices fresh root ginger

1 fresh or dried chilli or 10 ml
(2 tsp) peppercorns

60 ml (4 tbsp) sherry

bouquet garni of parsley, thyme
and bayleaf

2.5 ml ($\frac{1}{2}$ tsp) salt

1.6 kg (3$\frac{1}{2}$ lb) corn fed chicken

AVOCADO SAUCE

1 large ripe avocado

1 fresh chilli, seeded, finely
chopped, or a few drops
Tabasco

5 ml (1 tsp) Dijon mustard

2.5 ml ($\frac{1}{2}$ tsp) salt

100 g (4 oz) ricotta or curd cheese

50–75 ml (2–3 fl oz) sunflower oil

1 lemon

75–90 ml (5–6 tbsp) yogurt

TO SERVE

lettuce leaves

TO GARNISH

rings of fresh chilli or strips of
red and green pepper

In a large heavy-based pan, bring the onions, carrots and celery to the boil in the stock. Add the ginger, chilli or peppercorns, sherry, bouquet garni and salt. Add the chicken and simmer, covered, for 15 minutes. Take off the heat and leave the pan, still covered, at room temperature for 4–6 hours. The chicken will be cooked and remain moist and succulent.

Drain the chicken, skin and pat dry. Joint or bone and dice.

USING THE METAL BLADE: make the avocado sauce. Scoop the avocado flesh into the bowl and add the chilli or Tabasco, mustard and salt. Process until smooth then add the ricotta; process again and, when smooth, add the oil and lemon juice to taste, finally adding the yogurt. Adjust the seasoning and if the sauce is too thick, drip in a little degreased chicken stock or water. The sauce can be served thick like mayonnaise or thinned further to a coating consistency. If you have to make the sauce in advance, keep it covered with cling film, pressed down onto it.

To serve: arrange some lettuce leaves in a dish, place the chicken pieces on it and coat in the sauce. Garnish with chilli rings, if liked.
See illustration facing page 48

Walnut Stuffed Pears in Sweet Tarragon Sauce

A delicious combination of complementary flavours makes this a special salad. However, always make sure the walnuts are fresh before you use them. The sauce, which is produced with a special food processor technique, can be adapted in a number of ways and you will find it good on all sorts of sweet salads. You can alter its consistency by using semi-whipped cream or try it flavoured with mint on an almond-stuffed fresh peach, over mixed diced fresh fruit, or flavoured with ginger and chilli. *Serves 4.*

SWEET TARRAGON SAUCE
1 egg
$\frac{1}{4}$ tsp potato flour or cornflour
30 ml (2 tbsp) caster sugar
30 ml (2 tbsp) tarragon vinegar
**30–45 ml (2–3 tbsp) whipping
   cream**

75 g (3 oz) walnuts
a little fresh root ginger, grated
$\frac{1}{4}$ tsp curry paste
salt
pepper
squeeze lemon juice
4 medium-sized ripe pears

TO GARNISH
tarragon or cress leaves

USING THE METAL BLADE: make the sweet tarragon sauce. Process the egg and potato flour for at least 30 seconds until pale and thick. Put the sugar and vinegar in a saucepan, dissolve the sugar and bring to the boil; immediately pour down the feed tube while the machine is running. Process for about 1 minute until pale and moussey then return to the pan and heat gently, stirring all the time, until the mixture thickens. Turn immediately into a bowl and leave to cool. Stir in the cream until the mixture is a coating consistency.

USING THE METAL BLADE: process most of the walnuts with the grated ginger, curry paste, seasoning and a squeeze of lemon until it forms a paste. Peel the pears, leaving the stalks on if possible and remove the core through the base using an apple corer and a teaspoon. Stuff the hollow with the spiced walnut paste. To serve: set on a plate and spoon over the sauce to coat the pear completely. Using a knife, finely chop the remaining walnuts and use them to decorate the pears. Garnish with a few tarragon or cress leaves. Serve chilled. Do not assemble too long before serving or the pear will discolour.

French Bean Purée

When beans are large but not stringy, it makes a change to make them into a purée. Once processed, I like to add them to a little browned butter to which I have added a little grated lemon rind and juice. Browned in this way, a little butter gives a lot of flavour and you can make all sorts of vegetable purées most successfully like this. *Serves 2–3.*

500 g (1 lb 2 oz) French beans
a little summer or winter savory
25 g (1 oz) butter
**a little grated lemon rind
   and juice**
salt
pepper

Top, tail and string the beans, if necessary. Cook in salted water or steam until tender; drain well.

USING THE METAL BLADE: process the beans with the herbs until smooth, but not textureless.
   Heat the butter in a heavy saucepan over a moderate heat until brown. Add a little grated lemon rind and some juice (it will sizzle at this point) and at once add the purée; stir to heat through, season with salt and pepper and serve.

TABBOULEH (CRACKED WHEAT SALAD)

This Middle Eastern salad is made from boiled cracked wheat. Cracked wheat is known variously as burghul, bulgar wheat, bourgouri and pourgouri and is widely available at health shops and some delicatessens. Flavoured with generous quantities of chopped parsley and mint, the salad can be made quickly with the help of a food processor. Tabbouleh is often served by wrapping a spoonful in a lettuce leaf. For a less traditional recipe, you can add various raw vegetables, but take care with tomatoes and cucumber as they can exude moisture and make the whole salad rather wet if they are not salted and drained first and added at the last minute. Frying the cracked wheat with a little curry powder, as I do here, is not traditional either but it is very good. It's delicious served with Pitta Bread (page 86) and one or two of the dips in this book. *Serves 4–6.*

60–90 ml (4–6 tbsp) olive oil
5–10 ml (1–2 tsp) curry powder
   (optional)
150 g (5–6 oz) cracked wheat
1–2 spring onions
3 good handfuls parsley heads
1 good handful mint leaves
salt
pepper
45–60 ml (3–4 tbsp) lemon juice
$\frac{1}{4}$ medium-sized cauliflower,
   cut in florets (optional)
25–50 g (1–2 oz) black olives,
   stoned (optional)
lettuce leaves

Place 15 ml (1 tbsp) of olive oil in a heavy frying pan, heat gently and add the curry powder, if using it, and the cracked wheat. Toss over a low heat until the cracked wheat is toasted and just browning. Turn into a bowl and add 350 ml (12 fl oz) of water. Leave to soak for 30 minutes then turn onto a cloth or absorbent kitchen paper; squeeze dry and leave spread out to dry a little.

USING THE METAL BLADE: roughly cut the onions into the bowl, add the parsley heads and mint leaves and chop but not too finely. Toss with the cracked wheat adding salt, pepper, lemon juice and olive oil to taste. Toss in some of the cauliflower and black olives. Arrange some lettuce leaves on a serving dish, mound the tabbouleh on it and decorate with the remaining olives and cauliflower florets.

JUST HOT CARROT AND CELERIAC SHREDS

One of my favourite ways with young courgettes, carrots, turnips or celeriac is to grate them very coarsely then stir-fry them briskly until hot and barely cooked. They should be served quickly or they can become rather watery. Carrot and celeriac combine particularly well. The celeriac needs to be cooked immediately it has been grated or it will discolour. *Serves 4–6.*

---

350 g (12 oz) carrots, peeled
150 g (5–6 oz) celeriac root,
   peeled
50 g (2 oz) butter
a few drops vegetable oil
salt
pepper
5 ml (1 tsp) fresh chopped mint
good squeeze lime or lemon
   juice

USING THE COLESLAW CUTTER OR VERY COARSE GRATER: lay the carrots sideways in the tube and grate; then grate the celeriac. Meanwhile, heat the butter with the oil in a wok or large frying pan over a high heat until browning and fragrant; add the vegetable shreds and stir fry rapidly, tossing around the pan, for about 1 minute until heated through; season with salt and pepper and sprinkle with mint. Finish with a squeeze of lime or lemon juice if you wish and serve at once.

Cauliflower and Egg Salad with Anchovy and Olive Dressing

Main course salads are increasingly popular and this one, with its piquant dressing, is nice served at any time of the year, either warm or cold. *Serves 4–6.*

1 cauliflower
4–6 eggs
sprigs of watercress, parsley
   or any green herb for garnish
a few black olives

DRESSING
3–4 anchovy fillets or 5 ml
   (1 tsp) anchovy essence
5–6 black olives, stoned
1 clove garlic, peeled
small handful parsley or
   watercress heads
15 ml (1 tbsp) wine vinegar
pepper
60–90 ml (4–6 tbsp) best olive oil
salt, if necessary

Break the cauliflower into generous florets and steam until tender but still crisp. Refresh under cold running water and drain well.

Boil the eggs for 8–10 minutes. Plunge immediately into plenty of cold water to prevent blue rings from developing around the yolks.

Soak the anchovies, if you find them too salty, in a little milk or water for 5–15 minutes. Drain.

USING THE METAL BLADE: make the dressing. Place the olives, anchovies, garlic, parsley or watercress, vinegar and pepper in the bowl. Process until finely chopped then gradually add the oil to make a thickish dressing.

To assemble the salad: arrange cauliflower in a shallow dish. Peel and halve or quarter the eggs and set around the cauliflower alternately with black olives and sprigs of watercress or herbs. Spoon over the dressing and serve either tepid or cold.

Crisp Potato Mattresses

Grated potato cooked into a crisp little mattress is nice served with a steak, chop or cold meat or with a poached or fried egg. Use old potatoes and press out the excess juice well. A simple supper dish can be made by adding parsley, lemon thyme, lovage or chives and a little chopped ham and serving it with Tomato Sauce (page 43). *Serves 4–6.*

700 g (1½ lb) potatoes, peeled
1 medium onion, skinned,
   roughly cut up
50 g (2 oz) plain flour
2.5 ml (½ tsp) baking powder
2 eggs
5 ml (1 tsp) salt
pepper
vegetable oil or fat for frying

USING THE COARSEST GRATING DISC: cut the potatoes into lengthways strips and grate using medium pressure on the plunger. Turn into a colander or sieve and press well to extract all the excess juice.

USING THE METAL BLADE: place the roughly chopped onion in the bowl and chop with the on/off or pulse technique; add the flour, baking powder and eggs and process to mix. Combine this mixture with the potato shreds and season generously with salt and pepper.

Heat about 1 cm (½ inch) oil in a frying pan and, once hot, fry tablespoonfuls of the mixture over a medium heat for several minutes. Press flat, to ensure they cook through, turn and cook until brown on both sides. Drain on absorbent kitchen paper and serve at once or refry or heat in the oven later on.

Gratin Provençal

Not strictly Provençal but robust, earthy and gutsy enough to be so called. It is made of layers of potato, smoked bacon and fried onion, sauced with tomato, garlic, anchovy and herbs. The skins are left on the potatoes, which increases their flavour. This makes a satisfying lunch dish on its own or with a salad or can accompany a plain roast, steak, chop or liver dish admirably; in this case I might cut down or even leave out the smoked bacon. You can vary the recipe slightly by using olives instead of the anchovies and garlic sausage or cold meat instead of bacon. *Serves 4–6 as a main course.*

15–30 ml (1–2 tbsp) fruity olive oil

100–150 g (4–6 oz) smoked streaky bacon or ham, cut into thick lardons

75–100 g (3–4 oz) Cheddar cheese

350 g ($\frac{3}{4}$ lb) onions, skinned, halved

700–900 g (1$\frac{1}{2}$–2 lb) medium-sized potatoes, well scrubbed

1–2 cloves garlic, peeled

handful mixed herbs: plenty of parsley and celery tops, a little finely chopped rosemary, basil, lemon thyme etc

$\frac{1}{2}$–1 can anchovies

800 g (1$\frac{3}{4}$ lb) can peeled tomatoes or fresh tomatoes, peeled

pepper

Heat the olive oil in a frying pan and add the lardons of bacon or ham. Sauté gently, removing when they have rendered their fat and are light brown. Keep the oil in the pan.

USING THE STANDARD OR COARSE GRATING DISC: grate the cheese and set aside.

USING THE THICK SLICING DISC: slice the onions, using firm pressure. Heat the reserved oil in the pan and fry the onion in it for 10–15 minutes until soft and light brown. Slice the potatoes using medium pressure on the plunger.

USING THE METAL BLADE: place the garlic, herbs and anchovies in the bowl; chop roughly then add the can of tomatoes with only half their juice or fresh tomatoes and process until roughly chopped. Set aside.

Grease a 20–30 cm (8–12 inch) ovenproof gratin dish. Make a layer of half the potatoes then half the onions in it and scatter with the bacon; season with pepper and pour over half the tomato mixture. Repeat with the remaining potatoes, onion and tomato mixture and scatter with the cheese. Bake the gratin in a hot oven 200°C (400°F) mark 6 for about 45–50 minutes until the potatoes are cooked and the top is a good brown.

Parsnip and Onion in a Creamy Nutmeg Sauce

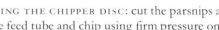

This is a vegetable dish which is prepared using the chipper blade. You can also use this recipe for potatoes, large carrots, celeriac, turnip, swede or aubergines. *Serves 4–6.*

500 g (1 lb 2 oz) parsnips
200 g (7 oz) onions, skinned
¾ oz (20 g) butter
salt
pepper

CREAMY NUTMEG SAUCE
25 g (1 oz) butter
40 g (1½ oz) flour
300 ml (½ pint) milk
salt
pepper
freshly grated nutmeg
butter

USING THE CHIPPER DISC: cut the parsnips and onions to fit crossways in the feed tube and chip using firm pressure on the plunger. Heat the butter in a deep frying or sauté pan, add the parsnips and onion and toss and sauté until glistening with butter and just beginning to brown; add about 300 ml (½ pint) of water, just to cover, and season lightly with salt and pepper. Boil vigorously for about 5 minutes while you prepare the sauce. Drain the cooking liquid into a measuring jug and turn the vegetables into a greased gratin dish.

USING THE METAL BLADE: place the butter, flour and milk in the food processor and process, adding in 200 ml (7 fl oz) of hot liquid from the vegetables. Once smoothly mixed, turn back into the pan and bring to the boil, stirring hard; add salt and pepper and flavour with a little freshly grated nutmeg. Pour over the vegetables. Dot with a few dabs of butter and grate a little more nutmeg over the top. Bake in a moderate oven 180°C (350°F) mark 4 for 20–30 minutes until the top is browned and the vegetables are cooked.

Cabbage with Apple and Cumin

This is an example of a nice chopped vegetable dish for which you can use a white winter or young green spring cabbage. You can vary the flavourings using caraway or fennel seed instead of cumin; you can leave out the apple or you can finish it with cream or yogurt, mixed with a little cornflour. You can use the same principle to braise kale, spring greens or spinach, adding a little fried smoked bacon or sausage. Try red cabbage instead of white with a little mixed spice and vinegar added. You can use chicken, duck or goose fat instead of butter or introduce olive or walnut oil for more flavour. *Serves 4–6.*

750 g–1 kg (1½–2 lb) white
    or spring cabbage
50–75 g (2–3 oz) butter
2 large eating apples, peeled,
    cored and quartered
¼–½ tsp crushed or ground cumin
    seeds
15 ml (1 tbsp) sugar
15–30 ml (1–2 tbsp) wine vinegar
salt
pepper

Cut the cabbage in half and remove the core; cut into 2–3 cm (1 in) slices, making sure none of the cabbage remains in solid chunks and toss into plenty of boiling salted water. Blanch for 1–3 minutes then drain and refresh with cold water. Drain very well.

USING THE METAL BLADE: melt the butter in a heavy casserole. Process the apples in the machine with the on/off or pulse technique until fairly finely chopped. Turn into the hot butter, sprinkle with the cumin and sugar and toss over a moderate heat for several minutes.

USING THE METAL BLADE: chop the cabbage in batches using the on/off or pulse techniques for even chopping and add to the casserole. Add the vinegar, salt and pepper and mix well. Either cook gently on top of the stove or place in a slow oven 170°C (325°F) mark 3 for 30–50 minutes. It can be prepared then left until the next day when about 1 hour in a slow oven will cook and reheat it.

SPICED BEAN FRITTATAS

Frittatas are like egg and vegetable drop scones and make a lovely summer dish hot, tepid or cold. These spiced bean frittatas have a gentle aroma of curry and are a nice way to use full size, but not stringy, French beans or leftover cooked beans. Serve as a first course alone or perhaps with a tomato sauce if hot or vinaigrette if cold. Or tuck into a roll for a spicy sandwich. You can make a variety of frittatas: how about spinach with a little Parmesan or mushroom or perhaps grated and squeezed courgettes with fresh herbs? *Serves 4–6.*

30–45 ml (2–3 tbsp) fruity olive oil
1 shallot, skinned, finely chopped
1 clove garlic, peeled, finely chopped
5–10 ml (1–2 tsp) curry powder
375–450 g (¾–1 lb) French beans, cooked, well drained
salt
pepper
2 eggs
a little olive oil, for frying

Heat the olive oil in a frying pan. Soften the shallot and garlic very gently in it. Sprinkle on the curry powder and fry gently for a moment.

USING THE METAL BLADE: chop the beans with the on/off or pulse technique until evenly and roughly chopped. Add in the oil, shallot and curry mixture, salt, pepper and eggs. Process until the eggs are well mixed and the beans evenly and finely chopped.

Heat a thin layer of olive oil in a frying pan, add tablespoonfuls of the mixture and fry over a medium heat, turning carefully once, until browned on both sides. Serve hot, warm or cold as a first course, vegetable or as a simple supper dish.

SPICED AUBERGINE AND PEPPER GRATIN

Quick to prepare and slow to cook, this dish is a marriage between an olive oil flavoured Mediterranean gratin and a spiced Indian dish. Lovely to eat hot, warm or cold it is substantial enough to make a good meatless main course if served with Pitta Bread (page 86) or a pilaf of rice and a salad. *Serves 4–6.*

1–2 aubergines
1 large green pepper, seeded
1 large red pepper, seeded
45–60 ml (3–4 tbsp) olive oil
2 medium onions, skinned, roughly cut up
2 cm (1 inch) cube peeled fresh root ginger
2–3 cloves garlic, peeled
10–15 ml (2–3 tsp) curry powder
2.5 ml (½ tsp) whole cumin seeds
15–30 ml (1–2 tbsp) tomato purée
2.5 ml (½ tsp) salt

USING THE THICK SLICING DISC: cut the aubergine into slices as thick as the feed tube width and slice with firm pressure on the plunger. Cut the peppers in half, pack the halves tightly together, stack tightly in the feed tube and slice with firm pressure on the plunger.

Take a shallow 25 cm (10 inch) ovenproof gratin dish and pour in 15 ml (1 tbsp) of the oil. Add the aubergines and peppers and toss together to mix.

USING THE METAL BLADE: place the cut up onions, ginger and garlic in the bowl and process with the on/off or pulse technique until finely chopped. Heat the remaining olive oil in a frying pan and, when very hot, add the cumin seeds and curry powder. Fry for a moment then add the minced onion, garlic and ginger; fry for a few minutes until just browning at the edges then add the tomato purée and fry for a further minute or two. Pour on 250 ml (8 fl oz) of water, add the salt, stir and pour over the aubergines and peppers.

Cover the middle of the gratin lightly with a butter paper or a piece of greaseproof paper and bake in a warm oven 170°C (325°F) mark 2 for 2½–3 hours until very well cooked, the excess moisture has all gone and the dish is browning around the edges. Serve hot, warm or cold.

PASTRY, PASTA AND YEAST DOUGH DISHES

You no longer need the traditional *tour de main* to be able to make good pastry all you need is your processor. It can make virtually any type of pastry from all-purpose to choux. For most pastries use the butter firm from the fridge so that you can incorporate enough liquid and then the pastry will roll easily without cracking and crumbling. For something a little different, why not try making sesame pastry, which I use in my Broccoli and Cream Cheese Quiche (below) or a mushroom-flavoured pastry, which is used for Mushroom and Nut Talmouses (page 64). Don't be afraid to experiment with different flavourings when you make pastry, pasta and dough; a touch of the right herb may turn the everyday into something rather special.

BROCCOLI AND CREAM CHEESE QUICHE WITH SESAME PASTRY

This pastry is flavoured with toasted sesame seeds and can be made with either plain or wholemeal flour. It has a lovely nutty flavour and can be used for many dishes. The light broccoli and cream cheese filling can be varied by using different vegetables like courgette, roasted pepper or leek while the flavour can be strengthened if you use strong Cheddar, Cambazola, Gruyère or a blue cheese. *Serves 4–6.*

SESAME PASTRY
30–45 ml (2–3 tbsp) sesame seeds
175 g (6 oz) plain or wholemeal
    flour
75 g (3 oz) firm butter, diced
good pinch salt

FILLING
175–225 g (6–8 oz) broccoli or
    calabrese, cooked
100 g (4 oz) full or medium fat
    curd cheese
3 eggs
50 ml (2 fl oz) milk
salt
pepper
nutmeg

Roast the sesame seeds in a covered, dry heavy frying pan, until they change colour and smell roasted. Cool.

USING THE METAL BLADE: place the flour, sesame seeds, butter and salt in the bowl. Measure out 45–60 ml (3–4 tbsp) of cold water, if using plain flour and 60–75 (4–5 tbsp) if using wholemeal. Process and add the water at once, stopping as the pastry draws into a dough. Knead briefly into a flat disc and chill, wrapped, in the fridge for ½–1 hour. Roll and line a 23 cm (9 inch) flan tin; prick the base, line with foil and baking beans and bake blind in a hot oven 200°C (400°F) mark 6 for 10–12 minutes until the pastry is set. Remove the foil and beans and continue baking for 10–15 minutes at 190°C (375°F) mark 5 until light golden and crisp.

USING THE METAL BLADE: process the broccoli until finely chopped then work in the cheese, eggs and milk. Season with salt, pepper and nutmeg and pour into the prepared pastry case. Bake in a moderate oven 180°C (350°F) mark 4 for about 20 minutes until the filling has just set. Serve hot, warm or cold.

MUSHROOM STUFFED PORK FILLET EN CROÛTE

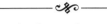

This rough puff pastry is quick and easy and I use it for both savoury and sweet dishes; Ginger and Apple Jalousie (page 68) can also be made with it. Wrapped around a pork fillet that has been stuffed with an interesting mushroom and Marsala duxelle, it makes a really good dinner party dish. *Cèpes* come in different sized packets; the one I use here is the 5 g (½ oz) one. *Serves 3–4.*

MUSHROOM STUFFING
45–60 ml (3–4 tbsp) Marsala, sherry or wine
5 g (½ oz) packet dried *cèpes* mushrooms, about 3–4 pieces
250 g (9 oz) mushrooms
1 shallot
small bunch fresh coriander or parsley
25 g (1 oz) butter
5 ml (1 tsp) crushed coriander seeds
salt
pepper

ROUGH PUFF PASTRY
40 g (1½ oz) firm, chilled butter
40 g (1½ oz) chilled lard
200 g (7 oz) plain flour
salt

450 g (1 lb) whole pork fillet
salt
1 egg, beaten

To make the mushroom stuffing: warm the Marsala and soak the dried mushrooms in it for 20–30 minutes. Drain, reserving the liquid, and cut off and discard any hard stems.

USING THE METAL BLADE: halve or quarter the fresh and dried mushrooms into the bowl, add the shallot and fresh coriander and chop finely with the on/off or pulse technique. Turn into a large piece of muslin and squeeze out the juice. Set this aside and use for the pastry, if you wish. Refrigerate.

Melt the butter in a wide, heavy pan and add the squeezed mushrooms to it; toss the mushrooms over a moderate heat for 6–8 minutes until dry and crumbly. Add the crushed coriander, mushroom-flavoured Marsala, salt and pepper and reduce again until dry. Cool.

To make the rough puff pastry: cut the butter and lard into little fingernail-sized cubes and chill well (a few moments in the freezer is a good idea).

USING THE METAL BLADE: place the flour and salt in the bowl and process for a moment to sift. Have 75 ml (5 tbsp) of iced water or reserved mushroom juice made up to 75 ml (5 tbsp) with iced water to hand. Add the chilled butter and lard, switch on and immediately pour the liquid down the feed tube. Switch off the moment the pastry draws together while the fats are still in pea-sized bits. Turn out onto a floured board, knead briefly together and roll to a rough 25 × 13 cm (10 × 5 inch) rectangle. Brush off any excess flour and turn the top quarter down to the middle and the bottom quarter up. Fold in two so that you have four layers and turn a quarter turn to your right. Roll and turn once more then leave to rest in a polythene bag in the fridge for ½–2 hours.

Trim the fillet, removing all sinew, skin and fat. Carefully cut the fillet nearly in half lengthways; then cut again lightly down the middle of each half and bat out flat under cling film. Place the mushroom stuffing down the meat and form into a long roll, tucking in top and tail ends.

Roll the pastry thinly and set the fillet in the middle, seam side up. Fold up the pastry to encase the fillet and seal with cold water, pinching the ends together; roll over onto a baking sheet so the seam is underneath. Mix a pinch of salt with the beaten egg to make an egg wash. Brush the pastry with egg wash, decorate with pastry leaves cut from the trimmings and carefully brush these with egg wash. Bake in a hot oven 220°C (425°F) mark 7 for 35–45 minutes. Serve hot cut in slanting slices. This is good with a leek purée served as a sauce or vegetable.

Kheema Samosas

These little parcels of spicy food can be encased in several layers of filo pastry or, as I've done here, in all-purpose pastry, a standby for quiches and all dishes needing a straightforward and crisp pastry. The filling can be made up of all sorts of ingredients like diced spiced vegetables, cream cheese and spinach or the kheema mixture with some added cooked peas and diced potato. *Makes 20 samosas.*

FILLING
50 g (2 oz) peas
50–75 g (2–3 oz) potato, diced
1 batch Kheema (page 42)

ALL-PURPOSE PASTRY
225 g (8 oz) plain flour
¼ tsp salt
100 g (4 oz) firm butter
vegetable oil, for frying

Either cook the peas and potatoes in with the kheema for the best flavour or cook and add to the ready prepared kheema. Cool before using.

USING THE METAL BLADE: make the pastry. Sift the flour and salt into the food processor. Add the firm butter, cut into hazelnut-sized cubes. Process, adding 60–90 ml (4–6 tbsp) of cold water as you do so. Stop when the mixture draws together into a lump. Knead briefly into a flat disc and chill, wrapped, in the fridge for 1–2 hours.

Divide the disc of pastry into 20 slices. Roll each into a ball then into a 15 cm (6 inch) circle. Cut the circle in half, take one half and moisten the cut edges; fold in half, sealing the edges together to make a cornet-shaped container. Stuff with a spoonful of cold kheema mixture, moisten the top edge and seal together firmly, pleating the top edge down. Prepare all the samosas this way.

Heat oil in a deep fat fryer, or to a depth of 4–6 cm (2–3 inches) in a wok, to 180°C (350°F). Fry the samosas, fairly slowly, turning once until they are a golden brown on each side. Drain on absorbent kitchen paper and keep hot or allow to cool and then reheat by refrying or placing in a hot oven.

Veal, Ham and Artichoke Pie

Old-fashioned veal and ham pies often had exotic additions such as sweetbreads, cock's combs, morels and even perhaps asparagus spears or artichoke hearts. Here I have processed a can of artichoke hearts in with the forcemeat which makes the mixture moist and gives an intriguing flavour. The hot water crust is easy to make in the food processor and the recipe is useful since it can be made several days ahead. For a good, moist pie you need fatty ham. If you can't get this, use ham or uncooked gammon and add up to 100 g (4 oz) of back pork fat. *Serves 8–10.*

HOT WATER CRUST
100 g (4 oz) lard
50 g (2 oz) butter
175 ml (6 fl oz) mixed milk and water
500 g (1 lb 2 oz) strong white flour
10 ml (2 tsp) icing sugar
5 ml (1 tsp) salt
1 egg

To make the hot water crust: roughly cut up the lard and butter and put in a saucepan with the milk and water. Bring to the boil.

USING THE PLASTIC OR METAL BLADE: place the flour, icing sugar and salt in the bowl; process for a moment to mix then pour the hot milk mixture down the feed tube in a steady stream and break in the egg. Process the mixture until it draws into a lump around the central column. Switch off. Turn into a bowl and leave, covered with cling film or a cloth, to cool for about 15 –30 minutes until it is malleable.

To make the filling: take about half the ham and a third of the veal and dice it into thumbnail-sized cubes. Sprinkle with ground mace, cloves, nutmeg, thyme, pepper and a little salt and set aside.

FILLING
500 g (1 lb 2 oz) fatty cooked ham
700 g (1½ lb) pie veal
good pinch ground mace
good pinch ground cloves
freshly ground nutmeg
5 ml (1 tsp) fresh thyme or lemon thyme or pinch dried thyme
pepper
salt
400 g (14 oz) can artichoke hearts, drained
50 g (2 oz) fresh white breadcrumbs
a little grated lemon rind
3 eggs, hard-boiled

Remove all gristle and sinew from the remaining veal and ham, cut up roughly and sprinkle with ground mace, cloves, nutmeg, thyme, pepper and a little salt. Divide into three equal portions.

USING THE METAL BLADE: drop a third of the roughly cut up meat down the feed tube onto the moving blade; process until fairly finely chopped then switch off and remove to a large bowl. Repeat with the second pile and add to the first in the bowl (large machines may do both batches at once). With your hands, combine the diced meats with this mixture, sprinkling on 15 ml (1 tbsp) or so of cold water and mix well together. Set aside.

Rinse the artichoke hearts briefly under cold water; drain and lightly squeeze. Process the remaining pile of meat then add the artichokes, the breadcrumbs and a little grated lemon rind and process until you have a smooth forcemeat.

To assemble: while it is still warm and malleable, set a quarter of the pastry aside to keep warm; this will be made into a lid. Turn the rest of the pastry into a 24 cm (9 inch) greased cake tin with a removable base; gently push it out to cover the bottom then press it evenly up the sides. It will slip down while it is too warm but as it cools it will stay, so keep drawing the pastry up until it completely lines the tin. Line the pastry with a layer of the artichoke forcemeat, pressed out thinly. Now lay the three hard-boiled eggs in the mould, laying them so that when the pie is cut you will get circles of egg. Pack the remaining filling around the eggs, pressing well down to pack firmly and make a dome in the centre of the pie. Roll or press the remaining pastry to a circle to fit the top of the pie. Moisten the edges of the pastry in the tin with water, set the cover in place and seal the edges very carefully. Mix a pinch of salt into the beaten egg to make an egg wash. Trim, decorate and brush with the egg wash. Make a hole in the centre and set a little foil chimney in the hole. Place a meat thermometer, if used, in the chimney and bake in a hot oven 220°C (425°F) mark 7 for 10–20 minutes until the pastry is a good brown and has set; then turn down to 170°C (325°F) mark 3 and continue to bake for 1–1½ hours to a meat thermometer reading of 75°C (170°F) or until the meat feels tender when pierced with a skewer plunged through the hole. Remove the cake tin sides and leave to cool. The pie is best served after a day or two when the flavour has had time to develop.

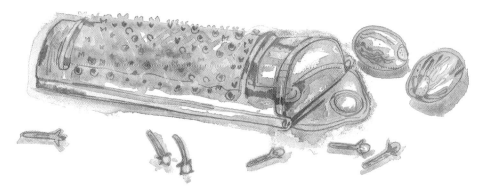

GOUGÈRES

This choux pastry flavoured with Gruyère cheese can be cooked in a large ring or made as individual puffs. They originate in Burgundy where they are traditionally served with Beaujolais. Hand them around hot with an apéritif or serve as a first course. *Makes 24–30 gougères.*

2.5 ml (½ tsp) salt
pepper
50 g (2 oz) butter, diced
100 g (4 oz) plain flour, sifted
75 g (3 oz) Gruyère cheese
3–4 eggs

Place 150 ml (5 fl oz) of water, the salt, pepper and diced butter in a saucepan and bring to the boil. Once the water boils, draw the pan off the stove, tip in the sifted flour all at once and stir until a ball of dough forms; return to the stove and cook, stirring, over a moderate heat for 1–2 minutes until a skin forms on the bottom of the pan. Do not beat. Remove from the heat and cool for 5–10 minutes.

USING THE STANDARD GRATING DISC: grate the cheese and reserve.

USING THE METAL BLADE: turn the mixture into the bowl, process and add the eggs one at a time; process for 30–45 seconds until the mixture is smooth and shiny then add the cheese, keeping back a little to scatter over the puffs before cooking. If possible, leave to cool before baking. Place the mixture well apart in generous teaspoon-sized blobs on an oiled baking sheet and sprinkle with the remaining cheese. Cook in a moderately hot oven 190°C (375°F) mark 5 for 15–20 minutes until brown and crisp enough not to collapse. Do not cook and dry out as much as you would normal choux buns. Serve at once or keep warm.

MUSHROOM AND NUT TALMOUSES OR TURNOVERS

Cream cheese pastry bound with mushroom juice (but also try yogurt whey or courgette juice) makes a crisp flaky cover for a mushroom and nut filling. *Makes 16 talmouses.*

225 g (8 oz) fresh mushrooms,
   washed and drained
1 medium onion, skinned,
   roughly cut up

CREAM CHEESE AND
MUSHROOM PASTRY
175 g (6 oz) plain flour
25 g (1 oz) firm butter
100 g (4 oz) full fat soft cheese
2.5 ml (½ tsp) salt
pepper
flour, for dusting
1 egg, beaten
sesame seeds (optional)

USING THE METAL BLADE: place the mushrooms and onion in the bowl and process with the on/off or pulse technique until fairly finely and evenly chopped. Turn into a large piece of muslin or cloth and squeeze out all the excess moisture (there should be about 60 ml (4 tbsp)); reserve and use in the pastry.

USING THE METAL BLADE: make the pastry. Place the flour, the butter cut into hazelnut-sized bits, cream cheese, salt and pepper in the bowl. Process and add the reserved mushroom and onion liquid until the pastry draws together and forms a lump around the central column. Knead briefly into a flat disc and chill, wrapped, in the fridge for 1–2 hours.

   To make the filling: melt the butter in a wide frying pan, add the chopped mushroom mixture and toss over a medium heat for about 6–9 minutes until the mixture has dried out and is crumbly.

Raspberry ice cream (page 82), Hazelnut crisps (page 92) and
Hazelnut ice cream with praline chunks (page 84)

FILLING

**chopped and squeezed
   mushroom and onion mixture**
25 g (1 oz) butter
50 g (2 oz) walnuts
1 egg yolk
good pinch ground mace
salt
pepper
cayenne

USING THE METAL BLADE: chop the walnuts with the on/off or pulse technique until fairly finely and evenly chopped; add the mushroom mixture, the egg yolk, mace, salt, pepper and cayenne and combine. Set aside until cold.

Roll the pastry out on a floured work surface until a little over 40 cm (16 inch) square. Using a ruler, trim the edges, mark off and carefully cut into 10 cm (4 inch) squares. Place a teaspoon of cold filling in the centre of each square. Make an egg wash by beating a pinch of salt into the egg. Moisten the edges with a pastry brush dipped in the egg wash and turn up opposite corners. Pinch together at the top, fold up the other two sides and seal all the edges to make talmouses. Alternatively, fold over to make triangular turnovers. Brush with egg wash and sprinkle with sesame seeds, if you wish. Lay on a greased baking sheet and bake in the oven at 200°C (400°F) mark 6 for 18–20 minutes until crisp and golden brown. Serve hot or cold.

WHOLEMEAL TARTLETS WITH PEA PURÉE, SMOKED BACON AND MINT CREAM

I use a crisp wholemeal pastry for these tartlets which are filled with a delicate pea purée and topped with a little minty whipped cream and diced smoked bacon—a very happy combination. *Serves 4–6.*

PASTRY

175 g (6 oz) wholemeal flour
5 ml (1 tsp) salt
**90 g (3½ oz) soft margarine,
   diced and chilled in the
   freezer**
flour, for dusting

FILLING

40 g (1½ oz) butter
**1 shallot or small onion, skinned,
   finely chopped**
700 g (1½ lb) frozen peas, thawed
¼ chicken stock cube
salt (optional)
pepper
2–3 sprigs fresh mint
1 egg
**15–30 ml (1–2 tbsp) double cream
   (optional)**
**175 g (6 oz) thickly sliced smoked
   streaky bacon, finely diced**
**few drops of vegetable oil
   (optional)**
**50–75 ml (2–3 fl oz) whipping
   cream**

USING THE METAL BLADE: make the pastry. Place the flour and salt in the bowl, add the diced chilled margarine and process, adding 45–60 ml (3–4 tbsp) of water until a soft dough forms. Turn onto a floured board, knead into 6 flat discs and chill in the freezer, wrapped for 1–2 hours.

Roll out each piece as thinly as possible and line individual tart tins. Prick, line with foil and baking beans and bake in a hot oven 220°C (425°F) mark 7 for 8–12 minutes until set; then remove the foil and beans and continue to bake in a moderately hot oven 190°C (375°F) mark 5 for a further 10–15 minutes until crisp, brown and cooked. Keep warm.

To make the filling: melt the butter in a heavy casserole and soften the shallot in it. Add the thawed peas with about 30 ml (2 tbsp) of their thawing liquid and a crumbled ¼ chicken stock cube. Season lightly with salt and pepper. Cover and simmer gently for 30–40 minutes.

USING THE METAL BLADE: process the peas with some of the fresh mint leaves; once smooth, add the egg and, if you wish, a spoonful or so of thick cream. Sieve the mixture, adjust the seasoning and keep warm in a bain-marie of hot water. Sauté the smoked bacon until golden and crisp, using oil if necessary. Drain well.

USING THE METAL BLADE: process the remaining mint leaves, the whipping cream and seasoning until stiff.

To serve: set the pastry shells on a serving dish, fill with hot pea purée, top with a blob of cold mint cream and garnish with diced hot bacon, a few shreds of mint leaf and some mange-tout, if liked. Serve at once.
See illustration on facing page

Wholemeal tartlets with pea purée, smoked bacon and mint cream (this page)

SPEEDY PIZZA

This pizza breaks many rules but wins through on taste, consistency and speed. After one rise, the very slack yeast batter is literally poured into tins with no rolling or shaping, the topping is added followed by a quick rise and into the oven it goes. Crisp, tender and succulent, topped with one of the garnishes suggested below, it is the favourite in our family. *Makes 4 × 20 cm (8 inch) pizzas.*

TOMATO TOPPING

350 g (12 oz) onions, skinned
30–45 ml (2–3 tbsp) olive oil
1–2 cloves garlic, peeled,
  chopped
30–45 ml (2–3 tbsp) tomato purée
400 g (14 oz) can peeled plum
  tomatoes and a 200 g (7 oz) can
  or 700 g (1½ lb) fresh, peeled
  tomatoes
8–10 fresh basil leaves or 2.5 ml
  (½ tsp) dried
salt
pepper

350 g (12 oz) strong bread flour
15 g (½ oz) butter or 15 ml (1 tbsp)
  vegetable oil
15 g (½ oz) fresh yeast
225 ml (8 fl oz) milk
1 egg
5 ml (1 tsp) salt

TO FINISH

1 can anchovies (optional)
50 g (2 oz) olives (optional)
100 g (4 oz) mushrooms
  (optional)
100 g (4 oz) prawns (optional)
50–75 g (2–3 oz) salami
  (optional)
4–6 artichoke hearts (optional)
100–150 g (4–5 oz) grated
  Mozzarella or Cheddar cheese
dried basil

The timing is crucial in this recipe so make sure that the topping is made and cooled by the time the dough has risen.

USING THE THICK SLICING DISC: make the tomato topping. Quarter the onions and slice them, using firm pressure on the plunger. Heat the oil and fry the onions for about 15 minutes until soft and golden. Add the garlic and tomato purée and fry for several minutes, stirring constantly until the purée smells roasted and darkens. Add the very roughly cut tomatoes and their juice and cook the mixture with a little seasoning and basil until it is thick and rich. Cool before using.

USING THE PLASTIC DOUGH BLADE OR METAL BLADE: make the dough. Place the flour, butter or oil and yeast in the bowl and process to rub in. In a jug, mix the milk and 100 ml (4 fl oz) of hot water to make a tepid mixture. Add the egg and salt to the bowl then, with the engine running, pour the liquid down the feed tube to make a slack batter. Process for about 45 seconds then set aside, in the bowl with the lid on, in a warm draught-free place (ideally, 27°C (80°F)) for about ¾–1 hour or until doubled in bulk. Alternatively, you can turn it into a large oiled bowl, pop it into an oiled polythene bag and rise it in that. Once risen, process again for 10–15 seconds, or knock back by hand if the dough is in a bowl; then pour into 4 well-oiled 20 cm (8 inch) sandwich tins or onto oiled baking sheets. Leave for 5–10 minutes only until the dough is just puffing (too long and the filling will sink through this soft dough) then spread the cooled tomato topping over the dough, but not right up to the edge. Decorate with either anchovies, olives, mushrooms, prawns, salami or artichoke hearts and sprinkle with the cheese and a pinch of basil. Leave to rise for about 10–15 minutes until the dough just puffs up around the edge of the tin. Bake in a hot oven 230°C (450°F) mark 8 for about 10 minutes until crisp and golden. Serve hot, warm or cold.

Fresh Herb Noodles with Courgette and Garlic

Fresh pasta can be made very easily with the help of a food processor. You can vary its colour and flavour by incorporating different vegetables or herbs. Any fresh herbs can be used; I like basil, parsley, celery leaf, watercress or chervil, but you might try chives, lemon thyme, tarragon or lovage and match them to an appropriate stir-fried vegetable. This pasta is so tasty that I like to dress it very simply, in this case just with stir-fried courgettes and Parmesan; you might also try stir-fried broccoli and smoked bacon, sliced mushroom and cream or squid and tomato.

Parmesan cheese is essential for pasta. The ready grated packets and tubs are often stale so try to buy Parmesan in the piece and grate it yourself. Some food processors have a Parmesan grater attachment so do use it. *Serves 3–4*.

PASTA
2 eggs
2 egg yolks
200 g (7 oz) plain strong flour
50 g (2 oz) fine semolina
a handful of watercress, parsley, chervil celery leaf or basil heads
5 ml (1 tsp) olive oil
2.5–5 ml ($\frac{1}{2}$–1 tsp) salt
flour, for dusting
10 ml (2 tsp) vegetable oil

STIR-FRIED COURGETTES
300–450 g (11 oz–1 lb) small courgettes
30 ml (2 tbsp) olive oil
2 cloves garlic, peeled and finely chopped
50 g (2 oz) Parmesan cheese
handful chopped herbs (optional)

USING THE METAL BLADE: make the pasta dough. Put the eggs and yolks into the bowl, add the flour, semolina, the well-dried leaves or heads only of the herbs, the oil and the salt. Process until the mixture resembles fine polystyrene-like granules. Continue processing for about 30 seconds to knead the mixture; if it begins to draw into one lump, add a little more flour; if it is very fine and powdery, trickle in a very little cold water. Don't try to process to a dough but once you have finished kneading, just press the mixture together in the bowl and you will find it will form into a ball. Turn onto a board and knead well. If you wish, rest the dough in an oiled polythene bag in the fridge for 30 minutes; the semolina will have absorbed more moisture by then. Pasta dough should be quite firm because if it is too soft it will stick together.

USING THE PARMESAN GRATER: grate the Parmesan cheese and set aside.

Divide the dough into two pieces (keep one in the bag for the moment) and roll out each piece as thinly as possible; dust with flour and roll up loosely. Then cut across into noodles and shake out onto a floured board. Alternatively, roll and cut using a pasta machine. The pasta can be kept on a tray for several hours or used straight away, but toss it occasionally to make sure it is not sticking together.

Bring a large pan of water to the boil, salt it and add the oil. Add the pasta and cook for 3–5 minutes until *al dente* then drain, not too thoroughly, keeping a little cooking water.

USING THE THICK OR MEDIUM SLICING BLADE: prepare the courgettes while the pasta is cooking. Slice the courgettes using medium firm pressure on the plunger. Heat the oil in a wok or large frying pan; when really hot, add the courgettes and garlic and toss around over a high heat until lightly cooked; add a handful of chopped herbs (optional). Add the cooked pasta with just a little of its cooking water and the Parmesan cheese. Toss together and serve at once.

GINGER AND APPLE JALOUSIE

This basic sweet pastry can be used for tarts, pies, turnovers or mince pies. Be sure to make it with firm butter so it is crisp and does not crumble. Here I have flavoured it with a little cardamom which enhances the ginger and apple filling. You can also try making this *jalousie* (so called because it looks like a louvred shutter) with the Rough Puff Pastry (page 61), sprinkling the pastry with cardamom and sugar as you roll and turn it. *Serves 4–6.*

SWEET PASTRY
175 g (6 oz) plain flour
30 ml (2 tbsp) icing sugar
¼ tsp ground cardamom
      (optional)
pinch salt
100 g (4 oz) firm butter
1 egg yolk
flour, for dusting
10 ml (2 tsp) demerara sugar
      mixed with pinch cardamom,
      for sprinkling

GINGER AND APPLE FILLING
700 g (1½ lb) cooking apples,
      peeled
50–75 g (2–3 oz) soft light brown
      sugar
15 g (½ oz) butter
about 3 nuggets of stem ginger
      in syrup, finely chopped
pinch ground cardamom,
      cinnamon and cloves

You can make the ginger and apple filling while you make the pastry but make sure it cools before you use it.

USING THE METAL BLADE: make the sweet pastry. Place the flour, icing sugar, cardamom and salt in the bowl and add the firm butter, cut into hazelnut-sized pieces. Process to the breadcrumb stage. Mix the egg yolk with 15–30 ml (1–2 tbsp) iced water. With the motor running, add this mixture but switch off, as the mixture combines into one lump. Turn onto a floured board and knead briefly into a flat disc before resting, wrapped, in the fridge for ½–2 hours.
   Peel, core and quarter the apples.

USING THE THICK SLICING BLADE: slice the apples then cook with the sugar, butter, finely chopped ginger and spices. Start cooking slowly, covered, but once tender and the juices have run, cook uncovered and stir frequently until the mixture is well reduced and keeping its shape. Cool before using.
   Roll the pastry and trim to 25 × 30 cm (10 × 12 inch). Cut lengthways into two with one piece a little larger than the other. Fold the larger piece in half lengthways and cut into the fold at 2 cm (¾ inch) intervals to within 2 cm (¾ inch) of the pastry edges. Spread the filling down the centre of the smaller piece, leaving 2 cm (¾ inch) clear all round. Moisten the edges with cold water then unfold and lay the louvred piece on top. Seal in place, brush with cold water and sprinkle with demerara sugar and cardamom. Bake in a moderately hot oven 190°C (375°F) mark 5 for 35–45 minutes until the pastry is crisp and brown.

PEAR AND RUM TART

Pâte sucrée, the rich crisp pastry which is so good for fruit tarts, is messy to make by hand and so simple in the food processor. You can fill the tart with any seasonal fruit and can use the pastry to make tiny tartlets. Flavour the crème pâtissière according to your fruit; you could use pear or raspberry *eau de vie*, orange zest or perhaps Grand Marnier. *Serves 4–6.*

PÂTE SUCRÉE
100 g (4 oz) very soft butter
50 g (2 oz) icing sugar
pinch salt
1 egg yolk
175 g (6 oz) plain flour
flour, for dusting

USING THE METAL BLADE: make the pâte sucrée. Process the very soft butter with the sugar, salt, egg yolk and 15 ml (1 tbsp) water until just mixed thoroughly. Sift in the flour. Process until just incorporated, turn out of the bowl onto a floured board, form into a flat disc and chill for 1–2 hours. Leave for a while at room temperature before rolling. Roll and line a 23 cm (9 inch) flan tin, prick, line with foil and baking beans and bake blind in a hot oven 200°C (400°F) mark 6 for 7–10 minutes. Once the

CRÈME PÂTISSIÈRE
225 ml (8 fl oz) milk
1 vanilla pod
50 g (2 oz) vanilla sugar
3 egg yolks
30 g (1¼ oz) plain flour or half flour and half rice flour or cornflour
15–30 ml (1–2 tbsp) rum (optional)
12 g (about ½ oz) butter

FILLING
150 g (5 oz) sugar
1 vanilla pod, split
6–8 ripe, firm pears
30–45 ml (2–3 tbsp) rum

pastry has set, remove the foil and baking beans and continue to bake in a moderately hot oven 190°C (375°F) mark 5 until fully cooked and a light golden brown with tiny bubbles of butter showing on the pastry. Cool on a rack.

To make the crème pâtissière: heat the milk in a heavy saucepan, add the vanilla pod and leave to infuse for 5–10 minutes.

USING THE METAL BLADE: process the sugar and yolks until pale then add the flour and process in. Remove the vanilla pod then pour the hot milk down the feed tube gradually, with the motor running, until smoothly worked in. Return the mixture to a heavy pan and bring to the boil over a moderate heat, whisking hard. Simmer for 2–3 minutes or until the flour has cooked and lost its raw flavour, whisking all the time. Rinse out the processor bowl. Return the mixture to the bowl with the metal blade and process until velvety, adding the butter and rum to taste. Turn into a bowl, cover and cool.

To make the filling: in a pan, dissolve the sugar in 600 ml (1 pint) of water. Add the vanilla pod and boil for 1 minute to make a syrup. Peel, halve and core the pears; slip them straight into the syrup and poach gently for 10–15 minutes until tender. Cool in the syrup.

To assemble the tart: drain the pears thoroughly. Stir the crème pâtissière well and spread over the base of the pastry. Place each pear half on a wooden board, cut side down and slice across thinly with a sharp knife. Do not disturb the slices but press the pear with your hand from the stalk end so the slices fall sideways. Carefully lift the complete sliced pear half on a palette knife and arrange on the crème pâtissière. Slice and arrange all the pear halves in the tart. Boil down a little of the syrup until thick, flavour with rum and brush over the fruit to glaze lightly.

COCONUT AND LIME PIE

The American biscuit crumb crust takes on a new style when made with creamed coconut which is combined with the crumbs in the food processor. Pressed into a tin and lightly baked, this sets to a light and delicious case which I have filled with a sharp lime mixture. *Serves 4–6.*

COCONUT-CRUMB CRUST

175 g (6 oz) digestive biscuits
2 Ryvita biscuits
100 g (4 oz) packet creamed coconut

LIME FILLING

3 large limes
30 ml (2 tbsp) cornflour
pinch salt
1 egg
2 egg yolks
100 g (4 oz) caster sugar
a drop or two of green colouring (optional)

USING THE METAL BLADE: make the coconut-crumb crust. Roughly break up the biscuits into the bowl and process with the on/off or pulse technique until crumbs begin to form. Stop and add the creamed coconut, cut in small pieces. Process until you have fine crumbs then tip the crumbs into a 23 cm (9 inch) fluted flan, tart or cake tin, which is about 5 cm (2 inch) deep. Mould and press the crumbs over the bottom and up the sides until it is evenly lined. Press well into place and bake in a moderate oven 180°C (350°F) mark 4 for about 10 minutes until golden. Press the base and edges again to firm the crumbs and leave to cool.

Finely grate the rind from 2 limes and squeeze the juice from all of them. Measure out 300 ml ($\frac{1}{2}$ pint) of cold water. Mix the cornflour with a little of the cold water. Combine the remaining water, the lime rind and juice and the salt in a saucepan and bring to the boil. Remove from the heat and stir in the slaked cornflour; bring to the boil again, stirring, and boil for about 1 minute until clear.

USING THE METAL BLADE: process the egg, yolks and sugar for about 45 seconds until thick and pale. With the machine running, pour the boiling mixture down the feed tube onto the eggs. Process for 30 seconds then pour all the mixture back into the saucepan and bring just to the boil while stirring all the time. Pour into the crust and leave to cool and set.

CREAM CHEESE AND FRUIT PIZZA

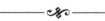

Continentals make fruit flans using a simple bread dough base so, I thought, why not make a sweet pizza. Using our speedy soft pizza base, try this cream cheese and lemon topped pizza, with or without sliced apple. *Makes 4 × 20 cm (8 inch) Fruit Pizzas.*

1 batch Speedy Pizza base (page 66)

TOPPING

225 g (8 oz) full fat soft cheese
100 g (4 oz) caster sugar
2 eggs
grated rind and juice 1 lemon
2.5 ml ($\frac{1}{2}$ tsp) natural vanilla essence
4 eating apples, sliced (optional)
cinnamon sugar (optional)
some apricot jam or redcurrant jelly, to glaze (optional)

Make up the pizza base (page 66). Pour this mixture into 4 tins or onto a prepared baking sheet; leave for about 5 minutes.

USING THE METAL BLADE: make the topping. Put the cream cheese and sugar in the bowl, work until smooth and add the eggs, lemon rind and juice and vanilla essence. Do not over-process or the mixture may curdle.

Spread this topping over the pizza base and, if using, cover with apples and dredge with cinnamon sugar. Bake in a hot oven 220°C (450°F) mark 8 for 10 minutes or so until crisp and golden. When baked, glaze, if liked, with apricot jam or redcurrant jelly.

WALNUT RUM PIE

The walnuts in the pastry echo the flavour of the filling which the rum and vanilla bring out admirably. Notice that the walnuts are processed with some flour—this is to stop them greasing too much. The filling is also good in an all-purpose pastry or a sweet pastry shell. *Serves 4–6.*

WALNUT PASTRY
50 g (2 oz) walnuts
150 g (5 oz) plain flour, sifted
75 g (3 oz) very soft butter
50 g (2 oz) caster sugar
1 egg yolk
15 ml (1 tbsp) cream or milk
pinch salt
flour, for dusting

FILLING
25 g (1 oz) chocolate
50 g (2 oz) butter
3 eggs
150 g (5 oz) soft dark brown sugar
75 ml (3 fl oz) whipping or single cream
45 ml (3 tbsp) rum
a few drops vanilla essence
100 g (4 oz) walnuts
pinch salt

USING THE METAL BLADE: make the walnut pastry. Process the walnuts with 15 ml (1 tbsp) of the flour until they are very finely ground, then set aside. Place the very soft butter, sugar, egg yolk and cream in the bowl and process briefly until just amalgamated; then add the ground nuts, sifted flour and salt and process briefly until just combined. Turn onto a floured board, pat into a disc and chill, wrapped, in the fridge for an hour or so to firm up. Roll and line a 23 cm (9 inch) flan tin (if the pastry has been in the fridge some time and is very firm, leave to soften a little before rolling). Prick the base, line with foil and baking beans and cook in a moderately hot oven 190°C (375°F) mark 5 for 10–15 minutes until the pastry has set. Remove the foil and beans and continue cooking at 180°C (350°F) mark 4 for a further 10 minutes or so until nearly cooked.

To make the filling: gently melt the chocolate and butter in a saucepan together.

USING THE METAL BLADE: process the eggs for about 1 minute until moussey. Add the sugar and process again. Now, with the engine running, add the butter and chocolate, the cream, rum and vanilla and switch off. Finally add the walnuts and process for a moment to chop slightly.

Turn the filling into the pastry case and bake at 170°C (325°F) mark 3 for 20–30 minutes until the filling has set. Serve hot, warm or cold.

SAVOURY AND SWEET SAUCES

Sorcery with sauces—there is no other word for the effects that can be achieved with the food processor. It can make classic sauces like Mayonnaise (below) and Sauce Gribiche (page 75) as well as producing new flavours and textures as in Leek Sauce Flavoured with Cream Coconut (page 74), Spinach and Mushroom Sauce (page 75) and Sweet Wine Mousseline (page 78). There are also various butters, both savoury and sweet, that can garnish a chop, add interest to a vegetable or enliven a pudding.

MAYONNAISE

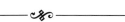

The food processor makes excellent mayonnaise. You can either use a whole egg or two yolks but make enough so that it does not get lost in the bottom of the bowl under the blades (some machines have greater dead areas, where food can remain unprocessed, than others). If using a whole egg, which makes a lighter mayonnaise, add the oil fairly slowly. If making it with two yolks, add the oil quicker to prevent the mixture from becoming thick and cloying.

Having mastered plain mayonnaise, you can start making variations by adding garlic or herbs, tomato, avocado, lime pickle, cream or yogurt or reduced fish stock. *Makes 300 ml ($\frac{1}{2}$ pint) mayonnaise.*

1 egg or 2 yolks
$\frac{1}{4}$–$\frac{1}{2}$ tsp salt
pepper
2.5 ml ($\frac{1}{2}$ tsp) Dijon mustard
5–10 ml (1–2 tsp) wine vinegar,
  lemon or lime juice
300 ml ($\frac{1}{2}$ pint) oil, half olive and
  half sunflower or safflower

Prepare all the ingredients before you start and let them come to room temperature.

USING THE METAL BLADE: place the egg or yolks, salt, pepper, mustard and about 2.5 ml ($\frac{1}{2}$ tsp) of vinegar in the bowl and process for about 20 seconds; then, very gradually, add the oil in a very fine thread while the engine runs. Once about half the oil is in and the mixture has taken and thickened, add the remaining oil in a fine trickle, faster for the yolks-only version; adjust the seasoning and add a little more vinegar. The whole-egg mayonnaise should just hold its shape while the yolks only version should be thicker. Add 5–10 ml (1–2 tsp) of boiling water to the yolks-only version to stabilise and thin it a little if you wish.

HALF AND HALF MAYONNAISE

This makes a nice light mixture that is not so rich or calorific as the classic mayonnaise. Chopped herbs, crushed garlic, tomato ketchup or Worcestershire sauce can all be added to flavour your sauce.

2 parts mayonnaise to 1 part
   yogurt
fresh herbs, chopped (optional)
garlic, peeled crushed (optional)
tomato ketchup (optional)
Worcestershire sauce (optional)

USING THE METAL BLADE: take the mayonnaise and process in to it half its quantity of yogurt and any additional flavouring; but don't process for long or it will thin out.

FOOD PROCESSOR CREAM

If you don't have any cream in the house, here is how you can make it in the processor from unsalted butter and milk. It cannot be whipped but is useful in puddings and ice creams, to enrich soups or finish sauces. *Makes 175 ml (6 fl oz) cream.*

100 g (4 oz) unsalted butter,
   chopped
60–75 ml (4–5 tbsp) milk

Put the butter and milk in a saucepan and heat just to melt the butter. Do not allow it to get any warmer than lukewarm.

USING THE METAL BLADE: turn the machine on and pour the mixture down the feed tube onto the blades; process for at least 30 seconds until it is all well amalgamated. Turn into a bowl and chill, stirring occasionally.

FRESH HERB AND GARLIC DRESSING

Blanching garlic makes it mild and delicate. In this dressing, you can use masses of cloves of firm, fresh garlic if you wish and any herbs you like. Try celery leaf, Florence fennel fronds, watercress or mustard and cress as flavourings. This mixture can be used to dress a salad or, because it is nice and thick, as a dipping sauce for vegetable sticks or Chinese leaves. *Makes 175 ml (6 fl oz).*

2–3 cloves garlic, unpeeled
a good handful of parsley, chervil
   or basil leaves or a
   combination of fresh herbs
5 ml (1 tsp) Dijon mustard
30 ml (2 tbsp) tarragon or wine
   vinegar
90 ml (6 tbsp) olive oil
30 ml (2 tbsp) whipping cream,
   yogurt or milk
salt
pepper

Throw the garlic into a pan of water and bring to the boil. Drain, peel the cloves and again place in cold water and bring to the boil; boil for 1 minute and drain.

USING THE METAL BLADE: place the garlic and herbs in the bowl with the mustard, wine vinegar, oil, cream, salt and pepper. Process together to chop the herbs and amalgamate all into a thick dressing. If possible, leave for a little while before serving for the flavours to blend and the mixture to thicken.

BASIL AND LIME MAYONNAISE

This variation of a classic mayonnaise, sharpened with lime and flavoured with basil, is particularly good with rich fish like salmon, turbot or even a tuna salad. Try it also with cold trout fillets, cold chicken salad or with hard-boiled eggs. *Makes 300 ml ($\frac{1}{2}$ pint)*.

1 whole egg
1–2 limes
salt
pepper
2.5 ml ($\frac{1}{2}$ tsp) Dijon mustard
300 ml ($\frac{1}{2}$ pint) oil, half olive and
   half sunflower or safflower
about 12 fresh basil leaves

USING THE METAL BLADE: break the egg into the bowl, add the grated rind of 1 lime, the salt, pepper and mustard; then add a good squeeze of lime juice and process for 15–20 seconds. Gradually add the oil in a fine thread until about half of it is in and the mixture has taken. Now add the remaining oil in a fine stream. Finally, add the basil leaves and more lime juice to taste and process until the herbs are finely chopped.

LEEK SAUCE FLAVOURED WITH CREAMED COCONUT

A vegetable purée can make an excellent sauce once it has been made utterly smooth in the food processor. I like to serve this leek purée, flavoured with creamed coconut, with chicken or shellfish or poached fish. For a simple supper you might try pouring the sauce over a poached egg, set on a slice of ham on a slice of granary toast. You can vary this sauce in endless ways with different combinations of cream, yogurt, cheese and various herbs. If you increase the quantity of leeks, without adding too much extra butter, you can make a lovely vegetable to serve with roasts, grills or chops. *Serves 4*.

300 g (11 oz) prepared leeks
50–75 g (2–3 oz) butter
salt
pepper
nutmeg
6–15 g ($\frac{1}{4}$–$\frac{1}{2}$ oz) coconut cream
75–100 g (3–4 oz) soft butter,
   cream cheese, curd cheese,
   yogurt or a combination of any
   of these (optional)

USING THE COARSE SLICING BLADE: slice the prepared leeks, drain well. Melt the butter in a heavy saucepan until sizzling, and toss in the leeks. Season lightly with salt, pepper and freshly grated nutmeg and cook gently, covered, for about 10–15 minutes until the leeks are quite tender and the moisture has gone. If too much liquid remains, turn up the heat and cook fast for a few minutes, stirring constantly.

USING THE METAL BLADE: process the leeks to a smooth purée, adding the coconut cream. You can serve the sauce like this but if you wish to turn the leeks into a really light and elegant sauce, keep adding bits of soft butter as the processor runs and you will get an Hollandaise-like sauce, based on a vegetable purée. If you use a proportion of light curd or cream cheese, process it in with the butter but do not process for too long or the mixture may curdle. If using yogurt, fold it in at the end.

SAUCE GRIBICHE

Sauce gribiche, often confused with sauce tartare, is excellent with fried fish dishes but is not to be despised with cold meat or hard-boiled eggs and it is positively sublime with pot-au-feu. *Serves 4–6.*

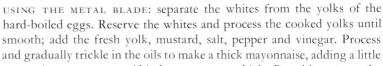

2 eggs, hard-boiled
1 egg yolk
2.5 ml (½ tsp) Dijon mustard
salt
pepper
10–15 ml (2–3 tsp) tarragon or
    white wine vinegar
225–300 ml (8–10 fl oz) oil, half
    olive, half sunflower, mixed
2 small cocktail gherkins
10 ml (2 tsp) capers
5 ml (1 tsp) caper liquid
small handful parsley heads
a little fresh, frozen or dried
    chervil
a little fresh, frozen or dried
    tarragon

USING THE METAL BLADE: separate the whites from the yolks of the hard-boiled eggs. Reserve the whites and process the cooked yolks until smooth; add the fresh yolk, mustard, salt, pepper and vinegar. Process and gradually trickle in the oils to make a thick mayonnaise, adding a little more vinegar or water if it becomes very thick. Roughly cut up the gherkins and capers, and add with the caper juice and the herbs. Process until finely chopped, adjust the seasoning and finally add the cooked egg whites; process just long enough to chop them slightly. Serve in a sauceboat.

SPINACH AND MUSHROOM SAUCE

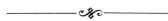

Use this purée of spinach and mushrooms, flavoured with rosemary, with fish, soft or hard-boiled eggs or ham. It has a delicate flavour that can be firmed up by beating in the cooking juices from smoked haddock, fish or ham. I rather like a dish of flaked smoked haddock and hard-boiled egg slices, covered generously in this sauce. You could also make it into a lovely vegetable dish by leaving it thick. Serve a poached egg on it or pile it into a dish with a border of brown rice. *Serves 4–6.*

100 ml (4 fl oz) milk
sprig rosemary
100 g (4 oz) firm button
    mushrooms
25 g (1 oz) butter
½ onion or shallot, skinned and
    finely chopped
salt
pepper
200 g (7 oz) cooked spinach
    (about 350 g (12 oz) fresh)
fish or ham cooking
    liquid (optional)
cream (optional)
butter (optional)
squeeze lemon juice

Pour the milk into a saucepan. Add the rosemary and heat. Leave to infuse, covered, until well flavoured.

USING THE STANDARD SLICING BLADE: pack the mushrooms sideways in the feed tube and slice using moderate pressure on the plunger.

Melt the butter in a small pan and soften the onion in it, add the mushrooms and sauté for 1 minute or so; then strain in the infused milk and simmer briskly, uncovered, for 10–15 minutes to cook the mushrooms and reduce the milk by half. Season with salt and pepper.

USING THE METAL BLADE: press excess moisture from the cooked spinach and reserve. Process the spinach to a purée, with the mushrooms, drained from their milk; once smooth, add the milk to make a thick coating sauce, adding the reserved spinach liquid if necessary. At this stage, you can add the cooking liquid from baked fish or ham or some cream or butter if you wish. Finish with a squeeze of lemon juice.

Turn into a saucepan and reheat before using.

Parsley Sauce

The food processor will whisk your white sauces or any of its derivatives to a velvet smoothness. And it really comes into its element when you want an enriched sauce; for up to 200 g (7 oz) of butter can be incorporated into this sauce which will then reheat happily, thanks to the processor's powers of amalgamation. You can turn this into a shrimp sauce by omitting the parsley. Add 100 g (4 oz) of peeled prawns to the finished sauce with a pinch of mace and a squeeze of lemon. Process just long enough to chop slightly. *Makes 300–450 ml ($\frac{1}{2}$–$\frac{3}{4}$ pint)*.

20 g ($\frac{3}{4}$ oz) butter
20 g ($\frac{3}{4}$ oz) plain flour
300 ml ($\frac{1}{2}$ pint) milk
salt
pepper
a handful of tender parsley heads
20–200 g ($\frac{3}{4}$–7 oz) butter, to enrich

Melt 20 g ($\frac{3}{4}$ oz) of butter in a saucepan, add the flour and cook, stirring, over a moderate heat for 1–2 minutes. Draw the pan off the heat, wait for the sizzling to stop then add all your milk (or any other liquid you wish to use). Whisk well and bring to the boil, whisking. Simmer for 1–2 minutes and season with salt and pepper.

USING THE METAL BLADE: chop the parsley heads then add a little sauce which helps them to chop finely. Once chopped, add the remaining sauce and process for about 30 seconds until very smooth and velvety. Enrich by adding butter in small cubes and, once amalgamated, turn back into the pan to reheat carefully. Never simmer an enriched sauce for long or it will separate.

Herb Butters

When you have fresh herbs by the handful in the garden, capture their flavours and preserve them. I have experimented with many ways of keeping the true flavour of fresh herbs and find one of the best is to trap the delicate essential oils in fat. Shavings of basil, tarragon or summer savory butter, tossed into your winter vegetables or on steaks or chops will bring back that fugitive summer note. Sometimes I use a lot of herbs and very little butter when I just want to preserve the herb in the freezer. At other times I add more butter when I'm going to use the mixture on baked potatoes, on vegetables or in a sauce. You can make *beurre aux fines herbes* by using 75 g (3 oz) of snipped chives, 50 g (2 oz) parsley, 50 g (2 oz) chervil and a sprig of tarragon to 100 g (4 oz) of butter. *Makes 225 g (8 oz)*.

100 g (4 oz) very soft butter
100 g (4 oz) fresh basil or parsley
   or summer savoury

Pick the leaves, flower buds and tender sprigs from the basil stalks.

USING THE METAL BLADE: place the chopped up butter and herb in the bowl and process until well creamed and finely chopped. Turn onto a sheet of cling film and roll into a long cylinder of 3–4 cm (1–1$\frac{1}{2}$ inch) in diameter; chill in the fridge or freeze before using.

PIQUANT BUTTER SAUCE

This sauce is based on that great favourite, Béarnaise, which you can make in exactly the same way as this. It is ideal with steaks, whole roast fillet or roast beef and we also like it with lamb. It is as good cold as it is hot, so it is wonderful with cold beef—and just try it in sandwiches or stuffed Pitta Bread (page 86). *Serves 4–6.*

2 shallots, roughly chopped
45 ml (3 tbsp) white wine
45 ml (3 tbsp) tarragon vinegar
15 ml (1 tbsp) fresh tarragon
    or 5 ml (1 tsp) dried
15 ml (1 tbsp) fresh chervil
    or 5 ml (1 tsp) dried
sprig fresh or pinch dried thyme
$\frac{1}{4}$ bayleaf
250 g (9 oz) tomatoes, peeled
salt
pepper
cayenne
100–175 g (4–6 oz) butter
2 egg yolks

USING THE METAL BLADE: place the roughly cut up shallot with the wine into the food processor and process with the on/off or pulse technique until finely chopped; turn into a small saucepan and add the vinegar, tarragon, chervil, thyme and bayleaf. Roughly cut up the tomatoes into the food processor and rough chop them with a few on/off turns. Add to the pan with a pinch of salt, pepper and cayenne. Simmer gently, stirring from time to time, until the shallot is tender and the liquid virtually all gone. Cook for a little longer, stirring constantly, until the mixture almost begins to catch and burn, thus bringing out the flavour.

USING THE METAL BLADE: turn the mixture into the bowl and process until smooth, adding 15–30 ml (1–2 tbsp) of water. Press through a sieve. Chop the butter into a pan and melt. If you are serving this sauce cold, make sure the butter only just melts because if it is too hot you can get a gritty texture when it becomes cold. To serve hot in a hurry, heat the butter until it is bubbling hot.

USING THE METAL BLADE: place the egg yolks in the bowl with the purée and process for 30 seconds before gradually trickling the melted butter onto the mixture. Once amalgamated, check the seasoning and turn the sauce into a bowl or sauceboat and stand it, covered, in a pan of hand-hot water 40°–45°C (100°–110°F). Leave to stand in a warm place for at least 30 minutes to give it time to thicken and for the flavour to develop; but you can keep it warm for an hour or more if you wish. Stir before serving. If the water is too hot, the yolks may curdle; if it gets cold, it is almost impossible to reheat.

ORANGE SPICE AND RUM BUTTER

Flavoured butters can be made so easily in the food processor; in fact, being able to cream the butter so soft and light allows one to incorporate more liquid than usual! This recipe with orange juice, spice and rum is nice used as a pancake filling or it can be served with steamed or baked puddings. *Serves 4–6.*

75 g (3 oz) very soft unsalted
    butter
25 g (1 oz) icing sugar or to taste
2 pinches mixed spice
1 orange
15–30 ml (1–2 tbsp) rum

USING THE METAL BLADE: process the butter with the icing sugar, spice and grated rind of half the orange until very soft and light. Gradually drip in the rum then about 30–45 ml (2–3 tbsp) of freshly squeezed orange juice. The mixture will only break and separate if the butter is not well creamed or if the liquid added is rather cold. Turn into a bowl and serve soft as it is or let it harden in the fridge before serving. It can also be rolled into a cylinder, chilled then cut into rounds or pretty shapes to serve from the freezer.

Sweet Wine Mousseline

This is the sort of sauce you make and use on the spot. It takes only two or three minutes to make and can be varied to suit your menu. Serve it with steamed or baked puddings, pancakes, ice cream or poached fruit. You can adapt the recipe, keeping the sugar, liquid and egg proportions about the same; instead of the wine, make an orange, lemon, clementine or passion fruit syrup or a simple sugar syrup flavoured with coffee, chocolate, almond essence or various liqueurs. *Serves 4–6.*

50 g (2 oz) caster sugar
75 ml (3 fl oz) sweet white wine
1 egg
1 egg yolk
$\frac{1}{4}$–$\frac{1}{2}$ tsp arrowroot, potato flour or
  cornflour (optional)

In a small saucepan, melt the sugar in the wine then boil fast for $1\frac{1}{2}$–2 minutes until it reaches 112°C (235°F) and forms a thread.

USING THE METAL BLADE: process the egg and yolk for a good $1\frac{1}{2}$–2 minutes until light and fluffy; then pour the boiling syrup down the feed tube in a steady stream with the engine running. Process for a further minute until thick and moussey then turn into a sauceboat and serve at once because it will separate and thin out relatively quickly after being made. If it is going to have to wait or if you want to serve it cold, thicken the syrup with arrowroot, potato flour or cornflour.

Herb Sauce for Fish

This is a Hollandaise-style sauce. It can be served hot with poached salmon, turbot or trout. This sauce can be made with just one herb like watercress, fennel or sorrel or you can create your own combinations. *Serves 4–6.*

175–225 g (6–8 oz) unsalted
  butter
2 egg yolks
15 ml (1 tbsp) lemon juice or to
  taste
15 ml (1 tbsp) wine vinegar
15–30 ml (1–2 tbsp) herbs, finely
  chopped e.g. fennel,
  watercress, sorrel or parsley
salt
pepper

Chop up and melt the butter gently in a pan.

USING THE METAL BLADE: process the egg yolks and add the lemon juice then the vinegar. With the engine running, gradually pour in the melted butter in a fine stream, rather like making mayonnaise. Add the herbs and seasoning and turn into a serving dish or jug. Stand this container, covered, in a warm place in a bain-marie of hand-hot water 40°–45°C (100°–110°F) and, in about 20–30 minutes, it will have thickened nicely and the flavour will have developed. It will keep for an hour or so without deteriorating. If the water is too hot, the yolks may curdle; if it gets cold, it is almost impossible to reheat.

FRUIT PUDDINGS, ICE CREAMS AND SORBETS

Pulp, cream or blend your fruits; the processor will do it all for you in double quick time. You can turn fruits into instant puddings, fools, crumbles or bases for ice creams and sorbets. For ice creams, the processor can make an egg mousse base, a custard base (without the dreaded cooking over gentle heat) or a fruit purée base. But perhaps the greatest strength in ice cream making is its ability to process a fairly firmly frozen mixture to a smooth ice cream, eliminating the stirring in and beating otherwise necessary when making ice cream.

TROPICAL PEAR OR ORANGE APPLE CRUMBLE

An exotic crumble, using tropical fruit juice with pears or orange juice with apple, which is quick to make. Crumble mixtures freeze well so make some up to have handy. *Serves 4–6.*

---

125 g (4½ oz) light soft brown sugar
grated rind and juice of half a lemon
2.5 ml (½ tsp) ground cardamom for pears or cinnamon for apples
150 g (5–6 oz) plain flour
¼ tsp salt
75 g (3 oz) firm butter
900 g (2 lb) medium-sized firm pears or cooking apples, peeled and cored
75 ml (3 fl oz) tropical fruit juice or orange juice

Grease a 20 × 25 cm (8 × 10 inch) shallow ovenproof dish. Mix the sugar, grated lemon rind and cardamom or cinnamon with 5 ml (1 tsp) of flour.

USING THE METAL BLADE: make the crumble. Place the remaining flour, salt, half the sugar mixture and the butter, cut into hazelnut-sized cubes, into the bowl. Process with the on/off or pulse technique until at the coarse breadcrumb stage. Do not process too finely. Place in a bowl while you prepare the fruit.

USING THE THICK SLICING BLADE: cut the pears or apples into quarters and slice using firm pressure on the plunger. Layer the fruit in the dish, sprinkling with the rest of the sugar mixture. Pour over the tropical fruit juice or orange juice and the lemon juice.

Sprinkle the crumble topping evenly over the fruit and bake in the oven at 180°C (350°F) mark 4 for 45–60 minutes until bubbling, brown and cooked through. Serve either hot or warm with Sweet Wine Mousseline (opposite) or custard.

LITTLE RASPBERRY CREAMS

You only need a small quantity of well-flavoured fruit purée to make these delightful creams which use half yogurt and half cream so are not too rich. They are very useful when you have a rather squashy mango, peaches that have been sat on or not quite enough raspberries to go round. Some fruits will need a squeeze of lemon juice to heighten their flavour and do try to choose a tasty natural yogurt because some are so synthetic tasting and floury. If you need to eke the creams out further or prefer a lighter mixture, fold in a whisked egg white at the end. *Serves 4–6.*

10 ml (2 tsp) gelatine
30 ml (2 tbsp) orange juice or water
175 g (6 oz) raspberries
about 50 g (2 oz) icing sugar
150 ml (¼ pint) whipping cream
150 ml (¼ pint) yogurt
5 ml (1 tsp) rose-water (optional)
squeeze lemon juice, if necessary

TO SERVE
raspberries (optional)
4–6 mint leaves (optional)

Sprinkle the gelatine onto the orange juice in a small bowl; leave to soak for several minutes then stand the bowl in a pan of hot water until the gelatine has melted.

USING THE METAL BLADE: process the raspberries to a purée with the icing sugar. Sieve and set aside. Place the cream in the bowl and process until thickening; then pour in the cooling gelatine and, once the cream is fairly stiff, stop and add the raspberry purée, the yogurt and rose-water. Process just long enough to amalgamate to a smooth mixture. Taste and add lemon juice, if necessary. Turn into glasses or small pots. Leave in the fridge until set then serve decorated with raspberries and a tiny mint leaf if you wish.

RHUBARB AND BANANA JULEP
WITH GINGER CREAM WHIP

This is so easy and absolutely delicious but make sure you use bright red sticks of rhubarb to get a clear pink colour. You also need to have really ripe bananas to counteract the acidity of the rhubarb. I call this a julep because I serve it in little glasses, topped with a swirl of ginger cream and decorated with tiny mint leaves. You could serve it equally well in a 600 ml (1 pint) bowl. *Serves 4.*

350 g (12 oz) pink rhubarb, sliced
1 slice from unpeeled orange
50–75 g (2–3 oz) granulated sugar
5 ml (1 tsp) gelatine
1 large ripe banana
1 nugget of stem ginger, cut up
15 ml (1 tbsp) syrup from stem ginger jar
150 ml (¼ pint) whipping cream
5 ml (1 tsp) caster sugar

TO DECORATE
mint leaves

In a covered saucepan, stew the rhubarb until tender with a slice of orange and sugar. Remove the orange slice and discard (it will take a lot of the acidity from the rhubarb). Sprinkle the gelatine onto 15 ml (1 tbsp) of cold water in a small bowl and leave for a few minutes until it forms a jellied cake.

USING THE METAL BLADE: roughly cut the banana up into the bowl and process until smooth. Measure out about 300 ml (½ pint) of warm juicy pulp from the rhubarb. Add it with the cake of gelatine. Process until smooth and the gelatine has melted then pour into 4 glasses. Chill in the fridge until it firms to a spoonable fool consistency.

USING THE METAL BLADE: place the cut up stem ginger and syrup in the bowl and process until chopped. Then add the cream and caster sugar and process for no longer than about 20 seconds, just until the cream is stiff enough to swirl on top of the rhubarb julep. Swirl or pipe onto the julep and decorate with mint leaves.

CHOCOLATE ICE CREAM WITH MINT CHIPS

Chocolate ice cream must be really chocolaty, which this is, and it also needs to be velvety smooth. I think you will find that this recipe, using a food processor, will give you a texture every bit as good as a professionally churned ice cream. *Serves 8–10. Makes about 1 litre (1¾ pints).*

45 ml (3 tbsp) cocoa powder
2.5 ml (½ tsp) instant coffee
100 ml (4 fl oz) milk
200 g (7 oz) best dark chocolate
500 ml (17 fl oz) whipping cream
2 eggs
3 egg yolks
30 ml (2 tbsp) honey
5 ml (1 tsp) natural vanilla
   essence
75 g (3 oz) mint matchmakers,
   roughly broken

Mix the cocoa and coffee powder to a paste with the milk in a heavy-based pan. Break up the chocolate and add to the pan with 300 ml (½ pint) of the cream. Heat very gently until the chocolate melts. Stir until smooth, and bring just to boiling point. While this is happening, process the eggs and honey in the machine.

USING THE METAL BLADE: process the eggs, yolks, and honey and vanilla essence for about 1 minute until thick and pale then, with the machine running, pour the boiling chocolate mixture down the feed tube. Process for about 30 seconds then switch off, stir in the remaining cream and turn into a shallow metal or foil container. Cool then freeze, stirring the sides into the middle once or twice as they freeze. Once the whole lot is fairly firmly frozen, chill a serving bowl or freezer container and roughly break up the chocolate mint matchmakers.

USING THE METAL BLADE: turn the mixture into the bowl and process until absolutely smooth. You may need to do it in several batches. Quickly process in the mint chips and pack the mixture into the chilled serving dish or freezer container. Mellow for about 20–30 minutes in the fridge before serving.

BANANA ICE CREAM

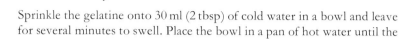

This is not a rich ice cream and it is a great favourite with my children. To get the best flavour, be sure to use really ripe bananas. *Serves 8–10. Makes about 1 litre (1¾ pints).*

2–3 ripe bananas
2 eggs
150 g (5 oz) icing sugar
⅛ tsp salt
⅛ tsp grated nutmeg
10 ml (2 tsp) gelatine
350 ml (12 fl oz) milk
500 ml (17 fl oz) whipping cream
15–22 ml (1–1½ tbsp) lemon juice

Sprinkle the gelatine onto 30 ml (2 tbsp) of cold water in a bowl and leave for several minutes to swell. Place the bowl in a pan of hot water until the gelatine melts.

USING THE METAL BLADE: process the bananas until smooth then add the eggs and sugar, salt and nutmeg and process again until well beaten. With the motor running, pour in the gelatine, while still quite hot, and then the milk, cream and lemon juice.

In smaller machines, you will have to stop once you have reached capacity; then turn the mixture into a bowl and stir in any remaining milk, cream and lemon juice. Turn into a shallow metal or foil container and freeze, stirring the sides into the middle as they freeze.

USING THE METAL BLADE: once the ice cream is fairly firmly frozen, process thoroughly in batches and turn into a chilled serving dish or freezer container and refreeze. Mellow the ice cream in the fridge for ¾–1 hour before serving.

RASPBERRY OR BLACKBERRY AND APPLE ICE CREAM

Apple adds a lovely texture to ice cream; however, I do not find it an entrancing taste on its own so I combine it with blackberries or raspberries. This is an example of an ice cream based on a fruit purée and from it you can develop and create your own recipes; try rhubarb and ginger, pear with macaroon, or blackcurrant with cassis. If your stewed fruit is syrupy, use it without its syrup. *Serves 4–6. Makes about 700–800 ml (1 pint 2 fl oz–1¼ pints).*

175 g (6 oz) caster sugar
100 g (4 oz) uncooked raspberries
   or 175 g (6 oz) cooked
   blackberries
300 ml (½ pint) drained,
   sweetened stewed apple
225 ml (8 fl oz) double
   or whipping cream
lemon juice, to taste

TO DECORATE
sprigs of mint

Place 100 ml (4 fl oz) of water in a saucepan, add the sugar and heat until the sugar is completely dissolved. Bring the syrup to the boil and boil hard for 1 minute. Cool.

USING THE METAL BLADE: process the raspberries or blackberries then add the apple and process again until smooth; pour in the syrup while the motor is running. Sieve the mixture then stir in the cream and add lemon juice to taste. Turn into shallow containers, preferably metal or foil. Cover and freeze, stirring the sides to the middle as they freeze.

USING THE METAL BLADE: once the ice cream is fairly firmly frozen, turn the mixture back into the food processor and process until very smooth. Turn it into a chilled bowl or container and keep in the freezer. Mellow in the fridge for ½–1 hour before serving. Decorate each serving with a sprig of mint.

See illustration facing page 64

APRICOT SORBET SPIKED WITH APRICOT BRANDY

A delicious winter sorbet can be made from dried apricots. Serve it in glasses with a little apricot brandy poured around it and hand amaretti or ratafia biscuits round with it. The recipe is for a generous amount as it stores well in the freezer. *Serves about 16. Makes about 2 litres (3¾ pints).*

650 g (1¼ lb) dried apricots
350 g (¾ lb) sugar
¼ tsp natural bitter almond
  essence (optional)
about 3 lemons

TO SERVE
apricot brandy (optional)
amaretti or ratafia biscuits

Soak the apricots in 1.5 litres (2½ pints) of water overnight; measure the soaking water and make it up to 1.5 litres (2½ pints) again. Add the sugar and gently simmer the apricots, closely covered, until tender.

USING THE METAL BLADE: purée and sieve the mixture, add the almond essence, if used, and lemon juice to taste (it needs to be quite sharp). Freeze the mixture in shallow foil or metal containers, stirring the frozen edges into the middle once or twice until firm. Chill a container.

USING THE METAL BLADE: process the mixture until absolutely smooth and pale, then turn into a chilled container and store in the freezer. Mellow in the fridge for 15–30 minutes until softened then scoop into well chilled glasses. Pour apricot brandy around the sorbet in the glass for those who wish it. Serve with amaretti or ratafia biscuits.

PASSION FRUIT SORBET

This sorbet is pure heaven. Passion fruit is now much more widely available than it used to be and this recipe transforms it into as smooth and velvety a sorbet as any professionally churned ice. You can use the syrup as a base for any flavoured sorbet that you fancy. You will need 100–150 ml (4–5 fl oz) of fruit pulp, so choose your fruits with this in mind. *Serves 4. Makes about 500 ml (17 fl oz).*

225 g (8 oz) caster sugar
100–150 ml (4–5 fl oz) passion
  fruit pulp from about 6–8 fruits
lemon juice, to taste

Place 600 ml (1 pint) of water in a medium-sized saucepan. Add the sugar and heat gently, stirring, until the sugar is dissolved. Turn up the heat and boil fast for exactly 5 minutes. Cool the syrup.

USING THE PLASTIC BLADE: cut the fruit in half and scoop out the pulp. Process to detach the pulp from the seeds. Gradually add some of the cooled syrup. Strain through a sieve, pouring the rest of the syrup over the pulp in the sieve and press really well to get all the flavour from the seeds and pulp. Add a little lemon juice to taste and turn into a shallow metal or foil container. Freeze, stirring the sides to the middle as they freeze. Chill a serving dish.

USING THE METAL BLADE: once fairly firmly frozen turn the sorbet into the bowl and process until light and pale. Turn into the chilled serving dish. This sorbet does not generally need much mellowing in the fridge before serving.

HAZELNUT ICE CREAM
WITH PRALINE CHUNKS

This is an extravagant recipe, but so delicious with its delicate flavour of infused hazelnuts, highlighted with chunks of hazelnut praline, that it's worth it. *Serves 4–6. Makes about 600–700 ml (1 pint–1 pint 2 fl oz).*

ICE CREAM
175 g (6 oz) hazelnuts
350 ml (12 fl oz) whipping cream
150 ml ($\frac{1}{4}$ pint) milk, scalded
1 egg
3 egg yolks
75 g (3 oz) caster sugar
$\frac{1}{4}$ tsp natural vanilla essence
pinch of salt

PRALINE
25 g (1 oz) caster sugar

Roast the hazelnuts on a tray in a moderate oven 180°C (350°F) mark 4 until golden right through or toast under a moderate grill, turning frequently. Turn into a cloth and rub off the skins. Reserve about 15 g ($\frac{1}{2}$ oz) for the praline.

USING THE METAL BLADE: make the ice cream mixture. Process the remaining nuts to a fine powder. Pour the cream into a saucepan, add the processed nuts and bring to the simmer. Leave, off the heat, to infuse for 10–15 minutes. Turn the nuts and cream into a muslin-lined sieve and squeeze out all the cream. Pour the hot milk over the nuts and squeeze again. Discard these nuts (if you like, you can dry them and add them to muesli). Pour the nut cream and milk mixture into a pan and heat to simmering point.

USING THE METAL BLADE: place the egg and yolks, sugar, vanilla and salt in the bowl and process for 30 seconds; pour the scalding nut cream down the feed tube and process for 45 seconds. Leave to cool and turn into shallow metal or foil containers for freezing. Freeze, stirring the sides into the middle several times as they freeze.

To make the praline: scatter the sugar in a thin layer over the base of a heavy frying pan. Heat gently until the sugar melts, runs and turns brown. Swirl the pan but do not stir the mixture. Place the reserved roasted, skinned hazelnuts on a piece of greased foil on a plate. Once the caramel is a good dark colour, pour it quickly over the nuts and leave until cold and brittle. Break up, place in a heavy plastic bag and crush to coarse lumps with a rolling pin. Sieve to remove fine powder which can be scattered over the ice cream on serving. (To make praline powder for cakes, process using the metal blade until finely powdered.)

USING THE METAL BLADE: once fairly firmly frozen, process the ice cream in the food processor until very smooth. Fold in the praline chunks. Turn into a chilled bowl or container and freeze. Mellow in the fridge for a little while if necessary before serving. Scatter with reserved praline powder if you wish.

See illustration facing page 64

BREADS, CAKES AND BISCUITS

Nothing can match that wonderful smell of freshly baked bread. With the help of your processor, you can savour it without the arm-aching task of kneading. The machine will mix and knead for you and all you have to do is watch the bread rise and eat it. Bread can be filled and baked, like the Rolled-up Onion Bread (page 88) or try making Middle Eastern Pitta Bread (page 86). The processor also mixes cake and biscuit mixtures in a moment to produce light sponges, soft and gooey chocolate cakes and moist fruit loaves.

LIGHT BROWN BREAD

An easy recipe for a moist brown loaf. The batter is slack, which allows you to make two loaves, even in a small machine. And once you have mastered it, start experimenting with different ratios of flour (look out for the wholemeal 'strong' flour which will give you a good rise on its own). *Makes 2 × 450 g (1 lb) loaves.*

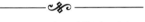

350 g (12 oz) strong white flour
25 g (1 oz) fresh yeast
30 ml (2 tbsp) honey
15 ml (1 tbsp) vegetable oil
150 ml (¼ pint) milk
50 g (2 oz) bran
15 ml (1 tbsp) sea salt
30 ml (2 tbsp) wheatgerm
225 g (8 oz) 100% wholemeal
    flour
flour, for dusting

Prepare two 450 g (1 lb) loaf tins.

USING THE DOUGH BLADE OR METAL BLADE: Place the white flour, crumbled yeast, honey and oil in the bowl and process to mix. Mix the milk with about 300 ml (½ pint) of warm water to make a tepid mixture. Gradually pour down the feed tube with the motor running to make a slack batter. Process for 30–45 seconds to knead. Wrap up the bowl and leave in a warm place for ½–1 hour at 20°–30°C (70–80°F) until doubled in size and almost filling the bowl. Return the bowl to the machine base, making sure that the blade drops into place, process to deflate then add the bran, salt, wheatgerm and most of the wholemeal flour. Process until the dough draws into one lump and detaches itself from the sides of the bowl, leaving them clean; add the reserved wholemeal flour plus a little more, if necessary, until this happens. Turn the dough onto a floured board and keep dusted in flour for it should be quite a soft dough. Knead briefly then divide into two. Press out each piece and roll up into a loaf, tucking the ends under; slash the top 2–3 times with a sharp knife and pop into the prepared loaf tins. Leave to rise inside a large oiled polythene bag or covered with a damp cloth in a warm place until the loaves have doubled in size. Bake in a preheated hot oven 220°C (425°F) mark 8 for 20 minutes then turn the oven down to 190°C (375°F) mark 5 for a further 20 minutes. At the end of the baking time, the loaves should sound hollow when tapped. Turn out and cool on a rack.

RYE BREAD WITH CARAWAY

The special flavour of rye flour, with or without the addition of caraway seeds or orange rind, makes this an attractive loaf. It cuts well and keeps well. *Makes 450 g (1 lb) loaf.*

225 g (8 oz) strong white flour
15 g (½ oz) fresh yeast
15 ml (1 tbsp) black treacle,
    molasses or dark brown sugar
175 ml (6 fl oz) yogurt or milk
175 g (6 oz) rye flour
2.5–5 ml (½–1 tsp) salt
grated rind half an orange
    (optional)
¼ tsp caraway seeds (optional)
flour, for dusting

USING THE PLASTIC DOUGH BLADE OR METAL BLADE: place the white flour, yeast and treacle in the bowl and process to 'rub in'. Mix 100 ml (4 fl oz) of hot water with the yogurt or milk so it is lukewarm. With the motor running, pour the liquid down the feed tube to make a slack batter and process for about 30 seconds. Now set the processor bowl in a warm, draught-free place for about ½–1 hour until the dough has doubled in bulk. Add the rye flour, salt, orange rind and caraway, if used, and process until the dough comes away from the outside of the bowl and forms a rope on the central column. Turn out onto a floured board and, keeping it dusted with flour, form into a loaf. Slash the whole length of it with a sharp knife and set to rise in a prepared 450 g (1 lb) loaf tin inside an oiled polythene bag in a warm, draught-free place. Once well risen and filling the tin, bake in a preheated very hot oven 230°C (450°F) mark 8 for 20 minutes then turn down to 190°C (375°F) mark 5 for a further 15–20 minutes. The loaf should sound hollow when knocked. Cool on a rack.

PITTA BREAD

Pitta bread is now readily available but is really at its best when freshly made. With the help of the processor it is easy to make and excellent with dips like Hummus, Mouamara or Roasted Pepper and Aubergine Dip (pages 19, 20 and 18). You might like to make it from half white and half wholemeal flour, in which case you need to vary the liquid quantity accordingly. *Makes 10–12 breads.*

450 g (1 lb) plain white flour
15 g (½ oz) fresh yeast
5 ml (1 tsp) salt
15 ml (1 tbsp) oil
vegetable oil, for greasing
flour, for dusting

USING THE PLASTIC DOUGH BLADE OR METAL BLADE: place the flour, yeast and salt in the bowl and process to sift. Trickle in the oil and then about 300 ml (½ pint) of tepid water to make a soft, pliable dough that comes away from the sides of the bowl. Add a little more flour if the dough is sticky or a little more water if it is too dry. Once mixed, process for about 30 seconds; then leave in the bowl to rise or form into a ball and place in a large bowl with a few drops of oil in the bottom; turn the dough in the oil then flip over, oily side uppermost. Leave the bowl inside an oiled plastic bag in a warm place for 1–2 hours until doubled in bulk. Reprocess or punch down, kneading briefly. Turn onto a floured board and form into a long roll then divide into 10–12 egg-sized pieces. Roll each piece into a smooth ball then roll out on a floured board to an oval shape about ½–1 cm (¼–½ inch) thick and about 20 × 15 cm (8 × 6 inch) in size.

Place these on greased and floured baking sheets, cover with a cloth and leave in a warm place for about 20 minutes until puffy. Bake in a very hot oven 240°C (475°F) mark 9 for 6–8 minutes without opening the oven door. They are done when puffed, speckled with brown and smelling cooked. Keep warm, wrapped in a cloth so they remain soft. Preferably eat while still warm though they can be rewarmed briefly under the grill. They can also be frozen and heated from frozen.

SOUTHERN CORN BREAD

This bread, from the southern states of America, is very quick to make and rather unusual. Eat it hot, spooned from the pan. It is good with rich stews, ragouts or baked vegetable gratins. I serve it on its own with plenty of Tomato Topping sauce (page 66) and some grated cheese and chives. If you prefer a less short bread, increase the flour to 200 g (7 oz) and decrease the cornmeal to 100 g (4 oz). Cornmeal is known as *polenta* in Italian shops and delicatessens. *Serves 4–6.*

---

150 g (5 oz) coarse yellow corn
   meal
150 g (5 oz) plain flour
15–30 ml (1–2 tbsp) caster sugar
15 ml (1 tbsp) baking powder
5 ml (1 tsp) salt
50 g (2 oz) butter, diced
1 egg
300–350 ml (10–12 fl oz) milk

Generously grease a shallow gratin dish or pan about 23 cm (9 inch) square.

USING THE METAL OR PLASTIC BLADE: place the cornmeal, flour, sugar, baking powder and salt in the bowl and process to mix. Add the butter and process to 'rub in'; now add the egg and milk and process for about 30 seconds until well mixed. Pour into the dish and bake in a hot oven 200°C (400°F) mark 6 for about 20–30 minutes until firm, brown and shrinking from the edges. Serve hot or warm from the pan.

SOFT YOGURT SCONES

Rather acidic yogurt is ideal for these scones though you could also use buttermilk, sour or ordinary milk. It is the acidity which helps them rise so you do not need to add an excessive amount of baking powder. A light touch is needed for making scones by hand and, similarly, your best results will come from developing a light touch with your processor, using only the lightest of on/off bursts once the liquid has been added. *Makes 12–15 scones.*

---

200 g (7 oz) plain white flour
100 g (4 oz) 100% wholemeal
   flour
2.5 ml (½ tsp) salt
7 ml (1½ tsp) baking powder
50 g (2 oz) butter, diced
50 g (2 oz) caster sugar (optional)
about 150 ml (¼ pint) yogurt and
   milk, mixed or buttermilk,
   soured milk or milk
1 egg, beaten

USING THE METAL BLADE: place the flours, salt and baking powder in the bowl and process briefly to mix well. Add the butter and the sugar and process to the breadcrumb stage. Mix the yogurt into the beaten egg. Pour this mixture into a ring on top of the flour and process briefly with the on/off or pulse technique for 2–3 two-second bursts, stopping to stir down or fork together. When the mixture is just amalgamated to a soft dough but before it is fully drawn together or smooth, turn it onto a floured board and lightly draw and pat together into a ball. Gently press this out with floured hands to a 2 cm (½ inch) thickness and cut out scones using a 6 cm (2½ inch) cutter. Lay on a floured baking sheet, sprinkle with flour and bake in a very hot oven 240°C (475°F) mark 9 for about 10 minutes. Cool on a rack and serve, preferably while still warm. These scones freeze and reheat well.

ROLLED-UP ONION BREAD

In this recipe, soft cooked onions and herbs are rolled into the dough to make an interesting savoury swiss-roll style of bread, lovely to eat warm with a country soup or rustic stew. I find that by rising a very slack dough to start with to get the yeast working, I get very good and quick results with a food processor. *Makes 1 loaf.*

200 g (7 oz) strong white bread flour plus extra if necessary
15 g (½ oz) fresh yeast
30 ml (2 tbsp) olive oil
5 ml (1 tsp) salt
5 ml (1 tsp) Italian seasoning or 2.5 ml (½ tsp) mixed dried oregano, sage and basil
200 g (7 oz) 100% wholemeal flour
vegetable oil, for greasing
flour, for dusting

FILLING
2 largish onions, skinned
10 ml (2 tbsp) olive oil
2 cloves garlic, peeled, chopped
5 ml (1 tsp) Italian seasoning or 2.5 ml (½ tsp) mixed dried oregano, sage and basil

USING THE DOUGH BLADE OR METAL BLADE: place the white flour in the bowl with the crumbled yeast and oil. Process to 'rub in' the yeast then trickle in about 275 ml (9 fl oz) tepid water with the motor running. Process to knead for about 45 seconds then set the bowl in a warm place, covered with a cloth until the mixture has doubled in bulk. Add the salt and Italian seasoning to the wholemeal flour then add to the soft dough, keeping a little back. Process until the dough draws from the sides of the bowl and forms one lump, adding more flour by spoonfuls down the feed tube until this happens; switch off. Turn the dough into a bowl with a few drops of oil in the bottom, turn it around then flip over so that the top is oily. Place the bowl in an oiled polythene bag or cover with a damp cloth and leave to rise in a warm place for about 1 hour until doubled in bulk.

USING THE THICK SLICING BLADE: make the filling. Halve and slice the onions in the processor. Heat the oil in a heavy frying pan, add the onions and cook gently over a low heat for 20–30 minutes until the onions are soft and golden, adding the garlic halfway through. Add in the Italian seasoning and cool.

Once the dough has risen, knock back by hand then turn out onto a well-floured board and knead briefly; press out with your hands to a 30 × 36 cm (12 × 14 inch) oblong. Spread with the cooled onion mixture and roll up lengthways. Pinch the ends together and lay seam down on a sheet of foil on the board. Flatten with your hand and slash the top diagonally at 2-cm (¾-inch) intervals to expose the onion filling. Leave to rise in a warm place until puffed and doubled in size then slide carefully onto a greased, hot baking sheet. Bake in a hot oven 230°C (450°F) mark 8 for 20–30 minutes until brown and cooked. Cool on a rack and preferably serve whilst warm and fresh.

COFFEE ALMOND CAKE WITH PRALINE ICING

This cake is made by creaming butter, sugar and eggs. The trick is to have the butter as soft as possible without melting and to process it for as short a time as possible once the flour has been added. This is a moist cake which keeps well. *Makes 20 cm (8 inch) cake.*

175 g (6 oz) soft butter
3 eggs
175 g (6 oz) caster sugar
135 g (4½ oz) self-raising flour
pinch salt
10 ml (2 tsp) powdered instant
    coffee
75 g (3 oz) ground almonds
60 ml (4 tbsp) milk

PRALINE ICING
50 g (2 oz) soft butter
150 g (5 oz) icing sugar
25 g (1 oz) caster sugar
15 g (½ oz) browned almonds

Prepare two 20 cm (8 inch) sandwich tins.

USING THE METAL BLADE: process the butter and sugar until creamed and pale (not too long or the blade will heat up and the mixture will get too soft). Add the eggs, one at a time, processing well. Stop and sift in the flour, salt and powdered instant coffee and then add the ground almonds and milk. Process with the on/off or pulse technique for 2–4 seconds, stopping to stir down, until all the ingredients are mixed.

Turn into the prepared tins and cook in a moderately hot oven 190°C (375°F) mark 5 for 25–30 minutes until springy to the touch. Test that it is cooked through by inserting a skewer; if it comes out clean it is done. Turn out and cool on a rack.

USING THE METAL BLADE: make the praline icing. Scatter the sugar in a thin layer in a frying pan. Heat gently until the sugar melts, runs and turns brown, swirling the pan, but not stirring the mixture. Pour the mixture over the hazelnuts on greased tinfoil and cool. Leave until cold and brittle, break up into the bowl and process to a powder. Set aside. Process the butter and sugar until smooth, add 30–45 ml (2–3 tbsp) of the praline powder and 5–10 ml (1–2 tsp) of water and process until soft and smooth.

Sandwich the cakes together with the praline icing.

CHOPPED DEVILLED NUT DROPS

These cheesy crisp biscuits are perfect for drinks parties or as a savoury. They are so quick and easy to make and you can vary the nuts you use. Make sure the butter is really soft for a very crisp, short biscuit. *Makes about 36.*

100 g (4 oz) strong Cheddar
    cheese
100 g (4 oz) plain flour
100 g (4 oz) very soft butter
¼ tsp curry powder
good pinch cayenne
50 g (2 oz) cashew nuts or
    other nuts

TO TOP
18 cashew nuts, split or other
    nuts

USING THE STANDARD GRATING BLADE: grate the cheese into the food processor.

USING THE METAL BLADE: add the flour and very soft butter, curry powder, cayenne and nuts to the bowl. Process using several on/off turns until the mixture draws into a paste. Form into marble-sized balls and place apart on a greased baking sheet. Press half a cashew or other nut into the centre of each, flattening it a little, and then bake in a moderate oven 180°C (350°F) mark 4 for 15–20 minutes until golden brown. Serve warm or cool on a rack and store in a tin.

SPICED CHOCOLATE CAKE

You can make this soft and spongy chocolate cake, reminiscent of an American devil's food cake, in the processor. It's a great favourite though I find that children prefer it without the walnuts. *Makes 20 cm (8 inch) cake.*

50 g (2 oz) good quality plain
   chocolate, broken up
50 g (2 oz) walnuts
175 g (6 oz) plain flour
25 g (1 oz) cocoa
175 g (6 oz) soft dark brown sugar
2.5 ml ($\frac{1}{2}$ tsp) baking powder
5 ml (1 tsp) bicarbonate of soda
5 ml (1 tsp) mixed spice
pinch salt
100 g (4 oz) very soft butter
100 ml (4 fl oz) plain yogurt
2 eggs
2.5 ml ($\frac{1}{2}$ tsp) natural vanilla
   essence
50 g (2 oz) sultanas

CHOCOLATE CREAM FILLING
50 g (2 oz) good quality plain
   chocolate, broken up
4–5 ml (3 tbsp) milk
50 g (2 oz) soft butter
275 g (10 oz) icing sugar, sifted
5 ml (1 tsp) natural vanilla
   essence
icing sugar

Prepare two 20 cm (8 inch) sandwich tins.

In a bowl, pour 100 ml (4 fl oz) of boiling water over the broken chocolate and leave to melt.

USING THE METAL BLADE: chop the walnuts roughly and set aside. Place all the dry ingredients in the bowl and process to sift and mix them. Add the very soft butter and yogurt and process until smooth. Add the eggs, melted chocolate and vanilla. Process again until smooth before finally adding the sultanas and roughly chopped walnuts; process only long enough to incorporate them. Turn into the prepared tins and bake in a moderate oven 180°C (350°F) mark 4 for 25–30 minutes until springy to the touch. Test that they are cooked through by inserting a skewer into the cakes; if it comes out clean, they are done. Leave for a few minutes before turning out onto a rack to cool.

Make the chocolate cream filling: set a bowl over hot water, place the milk and broken chocolate in it and stir until melted. Leave to cool.

USING THE METAL BLADE: process the butter until well creamed, add the sifted icing sugar, cooled melted chocolate and vanilla and process well together to a good spreading consistency.

When the cakes have cooled, sandwich them together with this filling and sift icing sugar over the top.
See illustration facing page 49

STRAWBERRY AND CREAM FILLED WHISKED SPONGE CAKE

The fatless whisked sponge defies the food processor but this method, using the food processor to whisk the yolks and sugar until a pale yellow and light, while you whisk the whites up by hand, is quick, neat and produces excellent results. Potato flour gives a particularly light result. *Makes 20 cm (8 inch) cake.*

50 g (2 oz) plain flour
20 g ($\frac{3}{4}$ oz) potato flour
4 eggs, separated
100 g (4 oz) plus 15 ml (1 tbsp)
   caster sugar
15 ml (1 tbsp) lemon juice

Prepare a 20 cm (8 inch) deep cake tin.

Sift the flours together two or three times. Put the egg whites into a bowl large enough to hold the complete mixture.

USING THE METAL OR PLASTIC BLADE: place the yolks and 100 g (4 oz) of the sugar in the bowl and process, adding in the lemon juice and 15 ml (1 tbsp) of boiling water. Process for two minutes or more until thick and

FILLING
450 g (1 lb) strawberries
300 ml ($\frac{1}{2}$ pint) whipping cream
a little vanilla sugar
about 30 ml (2 tbsp) kirsch
  (optional)

pale while you whip up the egg whites by hand until they hold a peak; whisk in the remaining 15 ml (1 tbsp) of caster sugar. Add the sifted flours to the processor bowl and process with the on/off or pulse technique for just long enough to combine. Gently fold this mixture into the whisked whites then turn into the prepared tin. Cook in a moderate oven 180°C (350°F) mark 4 for 30–40 minutes until springy to the touch and just drawing from the sides of the tin. Leave to cool for 4–5 minutes then turn out onto a rack and cool completely before cutting and filling.

USING THE THICK BLADE: set half of the strawberries aside for the top. Slice the remainder and set aside. Rinse and dry the bowl. Process the cream with a little vanilla sugar until thick.

Cut the cake carefully in half. Sprinkle the kirsch on one half of the cake then spread with the sliced strawberries; top with half the cream and cover with the remaining cake. Spread the top of the cake with the rest of the cream and decorate with the remaining whole strawberries. Leave in the cool, if possible, for 1–2 hours before cutting.

APPLE AND HONEY LOAF

Not quite a teabread and not quite a cake. My family certainly prefer this sort of fruity loaf to the richer, sweeter iced cakes. The honey, apple and clove give a lovely flavour and moist texture to this wholemeal loaf. *Makes 450 g (1 lb) loaf*.

225 g (8 oz) eating apples, peeled,
  cored and quartered
100 g (4 oz) soft butter
100 g (4 oz) soft dark brown sugar
30 ml (2 tbsp) honey, syrup,
  treacle or malt extract
2 eggs
200 g (7 oz) 100% wholemeal
  flour
2.5 ml ($\frac{1}{2}$ tsp) salt
7 ml (1$\frac{1}{2}$ tsp) baking powder
$\frac{1}{4}$ tsp ground cloves
50 g (2 oz) mixed peel or diced
  dried apricots (optional)

Prepare a 450 g (1 lb) loaf tin.

USING THE METAL BLADE: place the apples in the bowl and chop with the on/off or pulse technique until finely chopped. Set aside. Rinse out and dry the bowl.

Add the butter to the bowl and cream it until soft; add the sugar and honey and process again. Process in the eggs one at a time, stirring down if necessary. Mix the flour, salt, baking powder and ground cloves together and add to the bowl with the apples. Process just long enough to combine, stopping to stir down, then turn into the prepared loaf tin. Bake in a moderate oven 180°C (350°F) mark 4 for 40–50 minutes until just firm and a skewer inserted comes out clean. Leave in the tin for 10 minutes then turn out and cool on a rack. Serve sliced and buttered if you wish. This also makes a lovely pudding served hot with Sweet Wine Mousseline (page 78).

Peanut and Chocolate Chip Cookies

These American drop cookies, which end up as crisp short biscuits, are so easy and so good; having got the technique, you can vary the nuts—try hazelnuts, almonds, walnuts, pecans. Try varying the flavouring, too, with vanilla, cinnamon or spices. You can make them with salted peanuts if you use unsalted or lightly salted butter. *Makes 24–30 cookies.*

100 g (4 oz) plain flour
2.5 ml ($\frac{1}{2}$ tsp) bicarbonate of soda
2.5 ml ($\frac{1}{2}$ tsp) salt (omit if using salted peanuts)
100 g (4 oz) peanuts
100 g (4 oz) soft butter
50 g (2 oz) soft brown sugar
50 g (2 oz) caster sugar
1 egg
75 g (3 oz) chocolate chips

USING THE METAL BLADE: process the flour, bicarbonate and salt together briefly to sift and set aside. Process the peanuts with the on/off or pulse technique until fairly finely chopped and set aside. Process the butter and sugars until light and creamy; add the egg and process again, stirring down once. Add the chopped peanuts and chocolate chips, process briefly then add the flour mixture. Give two or three short on/off bursts of about 1–2 seconds each, stopping to stir down once and, if necessary, finish combining the mixture with a fork. Do not overprocess once the flour is in. Drop heaped teaspoons of the mixture onto greased baking sheets or roll into balls for perfect round biscuits and place about 8 cm (3 inch) apart. Flatten each cookie with the back of a fork and bake in a moderate oven 180°C (350°F) mark 4 for 12–18 minutes until pale golden. Some people like them still fairly chewy in the middle, others prefer them cooked absolutely crisp. Cool on the baking sheets for 1–2 minutes until firm enough to transfer to racks to cool completely. Store in an airtight container.

Hazelnut Crisps

These crisp, lacy biscuits are delicious served with ice cream and fruit puddings. They are so quick to make with the help of your processor. *Makes 24 hazelnut crisps.*

80 g ($3\frac{1}{4}$ oz) hazelnuts
100 g (4 oz) soft light brown sugar
30 g ($1\frac{1}{4}$ oz) plain flour
50 g (2 oz) butter, melted
15 ml (1 tbsp) crème de cacao or rum

USING THE METAL BLADE: process the hazelnuts with the on/off or pulse technique until roughly chopped; add the sugar and flour and process until fairly finely chopped before adding the melted butter and crème de cacao or rum; then switch off at once. Make teaspoon-sized balls of the mixture and set well apart on a greased or Bakewell covered baking sheet. Press to flatten then cook in a hot oven 200°C (400°F) mark 6 for a few minutes until they are light brown but be careful for they burn easily. Remove from the oven, leave 1–2 minutes to cool then, with the aid of a palette knife, remove the biscuits to a rack to cool and crispen. Store in an airtight tin.
See illustration facing page 64

GINGER AND SPICE SHORTBREAD

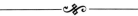

The lightest and most delicious shortbread can be made easily in the food processor. All you do is process the ingredients to a fine powder and press it down into a tin to bake. We make vast quantities every week to serve with coffee at our demonstrations. Here is a ginger and spice version but you can leave out all the spices for a classic shortbread. *Makes 24–30 pieces.*

---

225 g (8 oz) plain flour
5 ml (1 tsp) ground ginger
1.25 ml ($\frac{1}{4}$ tsp) ground cinnamon
pinch of ground cloves
pinch of ground nutmeg
75 g (3 oz) caster sugar
150 g (5$\frac{1}{2}$ oz) firm butter

USING THE METAL BLADE: place the flour and spices in the bowl and process for a moment to mix. Add the sugar and firm butter, cut into hazelnut-sized cubes. Process to a fine powder, stopping to stir down if it's not mixing evenly. Once no crumbs of butter remain (they will make tiny dark pools in the shortbread if not finely processed in), turn the mixture into a baking tin about 15 × 12 cm (10 × 8 inch) and press down evenly with something flat. Bake in a moderate oven 180°C (350°F) mark 4 for 20–30 minutes, depending on thickness, until pale golden and cooked right through; the buttery taste only comes through when the flour is thoroughly cooked. Remove from the oven, cut into fingers and leave for just a few minutes before removing from the tin to cool on a rack. Keep in an airtight tin.

INDEX